2nd
EDITION, REVIS

HIGH ALTITUDE BAKING

200 DELICIOUS RECIPES AND TIPS
FOR GREAT HIGH ALTITUDE
COOKIES, BREADS AND MORE

Edited by Patricia Kendall
COLORADO STATE UNIVERSITY EXTENSION

BOWER
HOUSE

DENVER

Cover, spot illustration, and text design by Margaret McCullough
Cover image courtesy of The Picture Pantry and Shutterstock

ISBN 978-1-917895-01-9

10 9 8 7 6 5

Grateful acknowledgment is made to individuals and publishers who have kindly granted permission for the use of the recipes in this edition of *High Altitude Baking.* If there are instances where proper credit has not been given, the publisher will gladly make necessary corrections in subsequent printings.

DISCLAIMER & LIMITS OF LIABILITY

CONTENTS

ACKNOWLEDGMENTS

The recipes and information in this book were developed by Colorado State University Extension and compiled from six high altitude baking bulletins published by Colorado State University Extension. The authors of each of the bulletins are listed below, with the original authors listed first, and the authors of subsequent revisions following:

Mile High Cakes:
1st edition: Elizabeth Dyar and Elizabeth Cassel, with technical assistance from Miriam Hummel, Elizabeth Twomey, and Elsie Slayton;
2nd edition: Ferne Bowman and Betty Lou Clithero;
3rd edition: Willene Dilsaver and Klaus Lorenz;
4th edition: Martha Stone, Pat Kendall, and Ingrid Hermanson.

Making Yeast Breads at High Altitudes:
1st edition: Klaus Lorenz and Willene Dilsaver;
Revisions: Pat Kendall and Colleen Burke.

Cookie Recipes from a Basic Mix for High Altitude:
Ferne Bowman, Edna Page, with technical assistance from Mary Frease, Marlene Gerlach, and Doris Trump.

Quick Mixes for High Altitude Baking:
1st edition: Ferne Bowman and Elizabeth Gifford;
Revisions: Pat Kendall

Today's Sourdough at High Altitude:
1st edition: Shirley Portouw with assistance from Ginger Allen, Alice Breshears, Sandra Childers, Goldie Gerber, Louise Haslem, Sherri Haslem, Donna Hellyer, Kay Kasza, Sue McCarthy, Edith Snowden, Noel Wilson, and Shirley Zabel;
Revisions: Shirley Portouw and Pat Kendall, with technical assistance from Martha Stone

High Altitude Baking:
Pat Kendall and Willene Dilsaver with technical assistance from Jennifer Anderson and Kathy Stubblefield.

FOREWORD

The challenges of high altitude food preparation have puzzled cooks living at high altitude since the early pioneers first pushed westward. Although many foods pose few problems, other than somewhat longer cooking times, recipes for baked goods developed at sea level (which include most every cookbook, newspaper and magazine recipe) can present a real challenge for cooks living above 3,500 feet.

The reason for most baking problems at high altitude is lower atmospheric pressure due to a thinner blanket of air above. At sea level, the atmosphere presses on a square inch of surface with a weight of 14.7 pounds. At 5,000 feet, there is only 12.3 pounds of pressure and at 10,000 feet, there is just 10.2 pounds of pressure– a decrease of about ½ pound per 1,000 feet. This decreased pressure affects food preparation in three related ways:

1. Leavening gases expand more quickly.
2. Moisture evaporates faster from foods.
3. Water and other liquids boil at lower temperatures.

In addition, because the climate of higher altitude areas is usually drier than that of lower altitude areas, flour may be drier and doughs may therefore require more liquid to reach the proper consistency. Most of the recipes in this book were developed at 5,000 feet and adjusted for use at 7,500 and 10,000 feet by researchers with the Colorado State University Experiment Station and Extension. The recipes in this book should yield good results over a range of altitudes as follows:

Recipes adjusted for 5,000 feet will work from 3,500-6,500 feet.
Recipes adjusted for 7,500 feet will work from 6,500-8,500 feet.
Recipes adjusted for 10,000 feet will work from 8,500-10,000+ feet.

In addition to the recipes created by Colorado State University Extension, a number of "signature" recipes have been added to the book to augment the various chapters. Although these recipes were not tested by CSU, they were created by high altitude culinary experts and professionals, and were tested. Credit is given to the creator of each "signature" recipe at the end of the given recipe. These recipes are adjusted only for use from 3,500-6,500 feet. Bakers living above 6,500 feet should refer to the guidelines given in the introduction to this book for adjusting the various types of recipes at their altitude.

To promote a healthier diet, many of the recipes in this book are lower in sugar and fat than comparable recipes found in many cookbooks. Some also feature fruits and vegetables for increased nutritional value and fiber. Nutritional information is provided for each basic recipe (see chart on page 180), and was calculated using fat-free (skim) milk. If whole milk is used, calorie and fat content should be increased accordingly.

We hope you enjoy *High Altitude Baking* and that it will become a book you pass down through the generations.

HAPPY BAKING!

Pat Kendall, PhD., R.D.
Extension Specialist and Professor
Department of Food Science and Human Nutrition
Colorado State University Extension

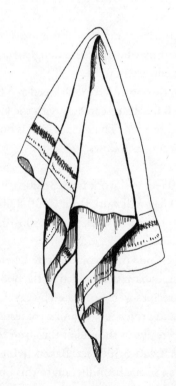

INTRODUCTION

At altitudes above 3,500 feet, the preparation of food may require changes in time, temperature or ingredients. There are no definite rules to use when modifying a sea-level recipe for use at high altitudes. However, at increased altitudes, recipes have been found to be more sensitive to slight changes.

Therefore, some general guidelines are worth consideration:

1. Read directions carefully before starting and follow them step by step.
2. Weigh or carefully measure ingredients with standard measuring equipment.
3. Use large eggs and double-acting baking powder.
4. When measuring flour and baking powder, spoon lightly into the measuring cup or spoon and then level off. Unless otherwise noted, flour does not need to be sifted before measuring.
5. Pack brown sugar lightly into the cup or spoon before leveling off.
6. Butter, margarine and shortening are best used softened, unless specified. Weigh or pack the specified amount into the measuring cup or spoon and then level off.
7. Instructions for the preparation of the baking pans are given with each recipe. Do not grease the sides of the pan unless specified. When baking cakes, the pan may be dusted with flour after greasing.
8. After cake batter or other thin batters have been poured into the pan, cut through the batter several times with a spatula or knife, or tap the pan lightly on a flat surface to release any trapped air so that you do not end up with air pockets in the finished product.
9. Using the proper oven temperature is a must for successful baking. Oven temperature regulators can vary, so it is always wise to check the temperature with an oven thermometer. If the temperature is either too high or too low, have the regulator adjusted by the dealer or learn what setting is necessary to obtain the correct oven temperature.
10. Bake batters and doughs in preheated ovens. For energy conservation purposes, preheat ovens only 10 minutes before baking.
11. Center pans in the oven. Do not allow pans to touch each other or the sides of the oven.
12. Baking times may vary depending on the accuracy of the oven. Remove a baked good when it appears done, whether or not the specified baking time has expired, then test for doneness as specified in the recipe.

13. Store cooled baked goods in a tightly covered container or a moisture/vapor-proof plastic bag to prevent loss of moisture. Label and freeze any portion of any product that will not be used within a few days.
14. Use any brand of enriched all-purpose flour (or cake or bread flour, if called for by the recipe).
15. Do not assume that a sea level recipe will fail. You may want to try it first, as it may need little or no modification.

ADJUSTING RECIPES FOR USE AT HIGH ALTITUDE

Yeast Breads: High altitude has its most pronounced effect on the rising times of yeast breads. At altitudes above 3,500 feet, yeast bread dough rises more rapidly and the rising period is shortened. Yeast doughs may over-rise if they are not watched carefully and allowed to rise only until doubled in size. Since the development of good flavor in bread partially depends on the length of the rising period, it is important to maintain that period. Punching the dough down twice lengthens the rising period, allowing enough time for the wonderful, nutty flavor to develop.

One other adjustment for bread baking at high altitude is a reduction in the amount of flour needed to yield dough of the proper consistency. Flour at high altitude tends to be drier and is thus able to absorb more liquid. Therefore, less flour may be needed to reach the proper consistency. No specific guidelines for the amount of the reduction can be given, however, because changes in humidity will affect the dryness of the flour and, subsequently, the amount needed.

Cakes: Most cake recipes developed for sea level need no modification up to 3,500 feet. Above 3,500 feet, decreased atmospheric pressure may result in excessive rising, which stretches the cell structure of the cake, making the texture coarse, or causing the cake to fall. This can usually be corrected by decreasing the amount of leavening, or by increasing the baking temperature by 15-25°F, which helps "set" the batter before the cells formed by the leavening gases expand too much. Increasing the baking temperature also helps compensate for the lower crust temperature and subsequent lighter crust color results from the faster evaporation of moisture at higher altitudes.

Excessive evaporation of water at high altitudes also leads to a higher concentration of sugar, which can weaken the cell structure. Therefore, sugar is decreased and liquid is increased when adapting sea-level recipes. Fat, like sugar, weakens cell structure. Rich cakes made at high altitudes may need less shortening, oil, butter or margarine (1-2 tablespoons per cup). On the other hand, because eggs strengthen cell structure, the addition of an egg to a sea-level recipe may help prevent a "too-rich" cake from falling.

Only repeated experiments with each sea-level recipe can determine the most successful proportions to use. However, the following "Cake recipe adjustment guide for high altitude" (Table 1) is a helpful starting point. Try the smaller adjustment first – this may be all that is needed.

TABLE 1: *Cake recipe adjustment guide for high altitude:*

Ingredient	3,500-6,500 feet	6,500-8,500 feet	8,500-10,000 feet
Baking powder – decrease each teaspoon used by:	⅛ teaspoon	⅛-¼ teaspoon	¼ teaspoon
Sugar – decrease each cup used by:	0-1 tablespoon	0-2 tablespoons	2½ teaspoons
Liquid – increase each cup used by:	1-2 tablespoons	2-4 tablespoons	3-4 tablespoons

Angel Food and Sponge Cakes: Angel food and sponge cakes present special high altitude problems. The leavening gas for these cakes is largely air. It is important not to beat too much air into the eggs used in these cakes. Beat egg whites only until they form peaks that fall over, not until they are stiff and dry. Overbeating causes too much expansion of air cells and leads to their collapse. Using less sugar, more flour and a higher baking temperature also helps strengthen the cell structure of these cakes.

Cake Mixes: Adjustments usually take the form of strengthening the cell walls of the cake by adding all-purpose flour and liquid. Suggestions for high-altitude adjustments are provided on most cake mix boxes.

Cookies: Although many sea level cookie recipes yield acceptable results at high altitudes, they often can be improved by a slight increase in baking temperature; a slight decrease in baking powder or baking soda, fat and/or sugar; and/or a slight increase in liquid ingredients and flour.

Biscuits, Muffins and Quick Breads: Quick breads vary from muffin-like to cake-like in cell structure. Although the cell structure of biscuits, muffins and muffin-type quick breads is firm enough to withstand the increased internal pressure at high altitudes without adjustment, a bitter or alkaline flavor may result from inadequate neutralization of baking soda or baking powder. When this occurs, slightly reducing the amount of baking soda or baking powder will usually improve the flavor. Quick breads with a cake-like texture are more delicately balanced and usually can be improved at high altitudes by following

Table 1: Cake recipe adjustment guide for high altitude (page 9). Characteristics of a quick bread that has not been properly adjusted for altitude include a porous, sugary crust; a coarse, gummy or oily texture; and a low volume in proportion to weight. These characteristics usually can be improved by a slight reduction in the proportion of leavening agents, sugar and fat, and/or a slight increase in the proportion of flour, eggs and liquid ingredients.

Pie Crusts: Pie crusts are not generally affected by high altitude. However, slightly more liquid may be used.

Cooking: The boiling point is the temperature at which the pressure of the water vapor equals atmospheric pressure and the bubbles of water vapor are able to break through the surface and escape into the air. If the atmospheric pressure is lower, the temperature required for water to boil is lower (see Table 2). Therefore, cooking food in water boiling at this lower temperature takes longer. A "3-minute egg" will take more time at high altitude, and a bowl of boiling soup is not quite as hot.

TABLE 2: *Approximate boiling temperature of water at various altitudes:*

Elevation	Sea Level	2,000 feet	5,000 feet	7,500 feet	10,000 feet
Temperature	212°F	208°F	202°F	198°F	193°F

Canning: Fruits, tomatoes and pickled vegetables may be canned in a boiling water bath. Because of the lower boiling point of water at high altitudes, increase the processing time by 1 minute for each 1,000 feet above sea level, if the sea-level processing time is 20 minutes or less. Increase the processing time by 2 minutes per 1,000 feet, if the sea-level processing time is more than 20 minutes.

Other vegetables, meats and poultry (low-acid foods) must be heated at

240°F for the appropriate time in order to destroy heat-resistant bacteria. A steam-pressure canner must be used to obtain a temperature of 240°F. At sea level, 10 pounds of steam pressure will produce this temperature. At altitudes above 1,000 feet, the pressure must be increased to compensate for the lower atmospheric pressure. See the following table for the pressure adjustments needed to reach 240°F using different types of pressure gauges:

TABLE 3: *Pressure required to reach 240°F:*

Elevation	Sea Level	1,000 - 2,000 ft.	2,000 - 4,000 ft.	4,000 - 6,000 ft.	6,000 - 8,000 ft.	8,000+ ft.
Dial gauge Pressure Canner*	10 pounds	11 pounds	12 pounds	13 pounds	14 pounds	15 pounds

* If using a pressure canner with a weighted gauge, use the 10 pound weight at altitudes of 0-1,000 feet. Use the 15 pound weight at altitudes of 1,001-10,000 feet.

Freezing: An important step in preparing vegetables for freezing is heating or "blanching" before packing. Heat vegetables for 1 minute longer than the time given for sea level if you live at or above 5,000 feet.

Syrup or Candy Making: To prevent excessive water evaporation, cook the syrup to a final temperature lower than that given for sea level. Lower the final cooking temperature by the difference in boiling water temperature at your altitude and that of sea level. This is an approximate decrease of 2°F for every increase of 1,000 feet in elevation (see Table 2). For example, at 5,000 feet, decrease the final temperature by 10°F from the sea level temperature.

Jelly Making: Use the same temperature correction as with syrup or candy making.

Deep-fat Frying: The lower boiling point of water in foods at high altitude requires lowering the temperature of the fat to prevent food from over-browning on the outside while under-cooking on the inside. The decrease varies according to the food being fried, but a rough guide is to lower the frying temperature by about 3°F for every increase of 1,000 feet in elevation.

Puddings and Cream Pie Fillings: Above 5,000 feet, temperatures obtained with a double boiler are not high enough for maximum gelatinization of starch. Therefore, use direct heat rather than a double boiler.

MILE HIGH
CAKES

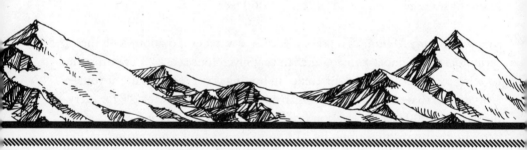

INTRODUCTION

High altitude cake baking presents many challenges. Cakes may rise too much and flow over the top of the pan, or they may rise and then fall. Or, the cake's texture may be porous and crumbly. The purpose of this chapter is to offer recipes for altitudes between 3,500-10,000+ feet, with each recipe working for a range of altitudes. The basic recipe for each cake recipe will work between 3,500-6,500 feet. Adjustments are given for altitudes of 6,500-8,500 feet and for 8,500-10,000+ feet.

As elevation increases, air pressure decreases and changes in recipes must be made to compensate (see Table 2 on page 8) However, contrary to popular belief, there is no set rule to use in modifying a sea level recipe for high altitude use. The modifications depend on the amounts of, and relationships between, the various ingredients of the original recipe. Therefore, we have designed recipes that are particularly suited to high altitudes and have not tried to modify the innumerable good recipes designed for sea level.

Ingredients: Cake flour is manufactured to produce light, tender cakes, and is used in most of the following cake recipes. Some recipes, however, specify the use of all-purpose flour. For best results, use the type of flour specified in each recipe. Double-acting baking powder was used in developing these recipes, but other types may be used. According to experiments in the Colorado State University Extension test kitchen, 1½ times as much single-acting baking powder as a given amount of double-acting baking powder will produce the same amount of leavening action. When butter, margarine or oil is used instead of shortening, mixing times should be slightly increased. It may also be necessary to decrease the liquid slightly.

Mixing Method: Electric mixers, both stand and hand, were used to develop the recipes in this chapter. Speeds recommended should be followed carefully. Use medium or high speed for creaming shortening and sugar, and for adding eggs. Use medium speed for beating egg whites. Use low speed for adding dry ingredients and liquid. Scrape down the sides of the bowl frequently with a rubber scraper during mixing.

BUTTERMILK CHOCOLATE CAKE
Makes One 9x13-inch or One 11x16-inch Cake

2	cups sifted cake flour
1¾	cups sugar
1	teaspoon baking soda
¾	teaspoon salt
1½	sticks (¾ cup) butter or margarine, melted
½	cup unsweetened cocoa powder
1	cup water
½	cup buttermilk
1	teaspoon vanilla extract
2	large eggs
	Chocolate Coconut Frosting *(recipe follows)*

Grease and flour a 9x13-inch baking pan or an 11x16-inch sheet cake pan. Sift together flour, sugar, baking soda and salt into a small bowl. Combine butter, cocoa and water in a small saucepan. Bring to a boil, then immediately remove from heat and cool slightly.

Preheat oven to 350°F. Combine buttermilk, vanilla and eggs in a large bowl. Stir in butter mixture. Stir in flour mixture until well blended. Pour batter into pan. Bake for about 20 minutes, or until a toothpick inserted in center comes out clean. Remove cake from oven and frost while hot. Slice and serve from pan.

CHOCOLATE COCONUT FROSTING

½	stick (¼ cup) butter or margarine, melted
2	tablespoons unsweetened cocoa powder
1	teaspoon vanilla extract
¾	cup powdered sugar
2-3	tablespoons milk
½	cup shredded coconut
½	cup chopped walnuts (optional)

Blend all ingredients together until smooth and of a spreading consistency.

CHOCOLATE RASPBERRY CAKE
Makes One Two-Layer 8-inch Round Cake

4	ounces semi-sweet chocolate
½	stick (¼ cup) unsalted butter
1⅔	cups sugar
3	large eggs
1	cup milk
1	teaspoon vanilla extract
1½	cups cake flour
¼	teaspoon salt
1	teaspoon baking powder
1	(10-ounce) jar good-quality seedless raspberry jam
	Chocolate frosting (recipe follows)
	Fresh raspberries and fresh mint, to garnish

Preheat oven to 350°F. Grease and flour two 8-inch round cake pans. Melt the chocolate (be careful not to scorch it); set aside to cool slightly.

Cream butter and sugar until light and smooth. Add the eggs, one at a time, beating after each addition, until well mixed. Add the chocolate; mix well. Combine milk and vanilla. Sift together flour, salt and baking powder. Stir the milk mixture and the flour mixture alternately, ⅓ at a time, into the butter mixture. Divide the batter between the pans. Bake for about 25 minutes, or until the middle of the cake springs back and does not indent when gently pressed. Remove cakes from oven and cool in the pans on a wire rack. While the cakes are cooling, make the frosting.

To assemble the cake: Run a knife around the rim of each cake pan and turn the cakes out onto a tray or baking sheet. Place the first cake on a plate; spread a thick layer of raspberry jam over it. Place the second cake atop the first. Using a narrow metal spatula, spread frosting evenly over the top and sides of the cake. Garnish with fresh raspberries and mint leaves.

CHOCOLATE FROSTING

2	tablespoons butter
6	ounces semi-sweet chocolate
⅔	cup sour cream
⅓	cup heavy or whipping cream
1	teaspoon vanilla extract
2	tablespoons powdered sugar

In a heavy saucepan, melt the butter and chocolate together (be careful not to scorch the chocolate). Remove from heat and pour into a bowl. Add the sour cream; mix well. In a separate bowl, combine the cream and vanilla. Mix the cream mixture and the powdered sugar alternately into the chocolate mixture, ⅓ at a time, mixing after each addition. Beat until smooth.

—Recipe courtesy of Melissa Craven

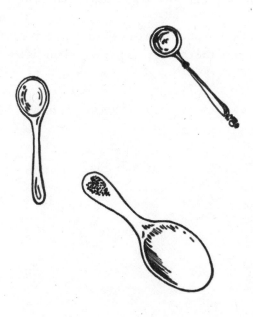

HOT FUDGE KAHLÚA CAKE

Makes One 8x8-inch Cake

1	cup all-purpose flour
¾	cup sugar
2	teaspoons baking powder
2	teaspoons cinnamon
4	tablespoons + ½ cup unsweetened cocoa powder
¼	teaspoon salt
½	cup milk
½	cup Kahlúa (or 2 tablespoons peppermint schnapps)
3	tablespoons butter, melted
1	cup packed brown sugar
2	cups boiling water

Preheat oven to 350°F. Stir together flour, sugar, baking powder, cinnamon, 4 tablespoons cocoa and salt into an ungreased 8x8-inch baking pan. Add milk, Kahlua and melted butter; stir well. In a small bowl, combine the brown sugar and the remaining ½ cup cocoa; sprinkle over the mixture in the pan – *do not stir!*

Pour boiling water over the top of the mixture in the pan. Stir 2 times only. Bake for 35 minutes, or until the cake is set and the pudding is bubbling. Serve hot with ice cream.

—Recipe courtesy of Melissa Craven

CHOCOLATE CAKE
Makes Two 9-inch Layer Cakes, One 9x13-inch Cake or 24 Cupcakes

2	cups sifted cake flour
½	cup unsweetened cocoa powder
1	cup sugar
2	teaspoons baking powder
⅔	cup vegetable oil
1	teaspoon vanilla extract
2	large eggs
1	cup milk

Preheat oven to 375°F. Grease and flour two 9-inch cake pans, one 9x13-inch baking pan or muffin cups. Mix and sift flour, cocoa, sugar and baking powder together into a bowl. Add oil, vanilla, eggs and milk; beat for 30 seconds with a mixer at low speed, scraping the bowl frequently. Beat for 7½ minutes more with a stand mixer at medium speed or 6 minutes with a hand mixer at high speed, scraping the bowl 4-5 times. Pour batter into pans. Bake for time recommended below, or until a toothpick inserted in center comes out clean.* Remove cakes from oven and cool in pans for about 12 minutes. Remove cakes from pans and finish cooling on a wire rack.

* Two 9-inch cakes: About 28 minutes.
  One 9x13-inch cake: Lower oven temperature to 350°F.
  Bake for 30-35 minutes.
  24 cupcakes (½-full): About 25 minutes.

ALTITUDE ADJUSTMENTS:
6,500-8,500 feet: Decrease baking powder to 1¾ teaspoons.
8,500+ feet: Decrease baking powder to 1½ teaspoons.
Increase milk by 1 tablespoon.

CHOCOLATE SOUR CREAM CAKE

Makes Two 8-inch Layer Cakes or 18 Cupcakes

2	squares (2 ounces) unsweetened chocolate
¼	cup hot water
1¾	cups sifted cake flour
¾	teaspoon baking soda
½	teaspoon salt
1½	cups sugar
3	large eggs
1	cup sour cream
1	teaspoon vanilla extract
	Cocoa frosting (recipe follows)

Preheat oven to 350°F. Grease and flour two 8-inch round cake pans or 18 muffin cups. Melt chocolate over hot water over low heat; cool. Mix and sift flour, baking soda, salt and sugar into a medium bowl. In a large bowl, beat eggs with a mixer at high speed until thick and lemon colored. Mix chocolate, sour cream and vanilla. Add chocolate and flour mixtures to eggs. Beat for 30 seconds on low speed, scraping bowl frequently. Beat for 3 minutes on medium-high speed with a stand mixer or 3 minutes at high speed with a hand mixer, scraping bowl several times. Pour batter into pans or muffin cups. Bake for time recommended below, or until a toothpick inserted into center comes out clean.* Remove cakes from oven and cool in pans for about 12 minutes. Remove cakes from pan and finish cooling on a wire rack. Frost with cocoa frosting, if desired.

* Two 8-inch cakes: 27-32 minutes.
18 cupcakes (½-full): about 29 minutes.

ALTITUDE ADJUSTMENTS:
6,500-8,500 feet: Decrease baking soda to ⅝ teaspoon.
Raise oven temperature to 375°F.
8,500+ feet: Decrease baking soda to ½ teaspoon.
Raise oven temperature to 375°F.

COCOA FROSTING

⅓ cup unsweetened cocoa powder
1⅔ cups powdered sugar
⅓ cup butter or margarine, softened
3-4 tablespoons milk

Sift together cocoa and powdered sugar. Add butter and milk; stir until well blended and thick enough to spread.

CHOCOLATE APPLESAUCE CAKE
Makes One 9x13-inch Cake

An easy, versatile cake.

2 cups cake flour
½ cup unsweetened cocoa powder
1 teaspoon baking powder
½ teaspoon baking soda
1¼ cups sugar
½ teaspoon salt
1 teaspoon cinnamon
½ cup vegetable oil
2 large eggs
1¼ cups applesauce
1 teaspoon vanilla extract
½ cup chopped nuts (optional)

Preheat oven to 375°F. Grease the bottom of a 9x13-inch baking pan. Sift together flour, cocoa, baking powder, baking soda, sugar, salt and cinnamon into a large bowl. Add oil, eggs, applesauce and vanilla; beat at medium speed until well blended, about 2 minutes. Stir in nuts, if desired. Pour batter into pan. Bake for 30-35 minutes, or until a toothpick inserted in center comes out clean. Remove from oven and cool in pan on a wire rack. Frost or sprinkle with powdered sugar, if desired and serve from pan.

TROPICAL CAKE
Makes One 9x13-inch Cake

1½   cups white sugar
1   teaspoon baking soda
2   cups + 2 tablespoons cake flour
2   large eggs, slightly beaten
½   teaspoon vanilla extract
1   (20-ounce) can crushed pineapple, undrained
1   cup chopped cashews
¾   cup sweetened flaked coconut, plus more
     for topping the cake
     Topping (recipe follows)
     Chopped cashews

Preheat oven to 350°F. Grease a 9x13-inch baking pan. In a large bowl, combine sugar, soda and flour. Stir in eggs, vanilla and undrained pineapple. Add cashews and ¾ cup of coconut. Pour batter into pan. Bake for 35-40 minutes. Remove the cake from the oven and cool in the pan. Spread the topping over the cooled cake. Sprinkle with coconut and chopped cashews. Refrigerate until serving.

TOPPING
1   (3.4-ounce) package instant vanilla pudding mix
1   (8-ounce) package cream cheese, softened
1   (8-ounce) container frozen whipped topping, thawed

Prepare pudding according to package directions; set aside. In a medium bowl, beat cream cheese until smooth. Mix in the prepared pudding. Fold in the whipped topping.

—Recipe courtesy of the Wheat Foods Council

ANGEL FOOD CAKE
Makes One 10-inch Tube Cake

1	cup + 1 tablespoon sifted cake flour
1	cup + ½ cup sugar
12	large egg whites
¼	teaspoon salt
2	teaspoons cream of tartar
½	teaspoon vanilla extract
½	teaspoon almond extract

Preheat oven to 375°F. Sift flour and 1 cup of sugar together 3 times into a bowl. In a separate bowl, beat egg whites, salt and cream tartar with a mixer at high speed until soft peaks (that barely fall over) form. With mixer running at low speed, slowly add the remaining ½ cup of sugar close to the beaters. Add vanilla and almond extracts; beat until stiff (but not dry) peaks form. Add flour mixture to egg white mixture, ¼ at a time, mixing at low speed for 10 seconds after each of the first 3 additions and for 20 seconds after the last addition. Scrape the bowl constantly during mixing. Pour batter into an ungreased 10-inch tube pan. Bake for about 35 minutes, or until a toothpick inserted in the center comes out clean. Remove cake from oven and cool in inverted pan.

VARIATIONS:
- CHOCOLATE ANGEL FOOD CAKE: Omit almond extract. Increase vanilla extract to 1½ teaspoons. Substitute ¼ cup sifted unsweetened cocoa powder for ¼ cup of cake flour.
- SPICE ANGEL FOOD CAKE: Sift with the flour: ½ teaspoon nutmeg, ¼ teaspoon ground cloves and 1 teaspoon cinnamon. Omit vanilla and almond extracts.

ALTITUDE ADJUSTMENTS:
6,500-8,500 feet: Increase flour to 1 cup + 3 tablespoons. Decrease the 1 cup of sugar to ¾ cup + 2 tablespoons.
8,500+ feet: Increase flour to 1¼ cups. Decrease the 1 cup of sugar to ¾ cup. Raise oven temperature to 400°F.

CHIFFON CAKE
Makes One 10-inch Tube Cake

2½	cups sifted cake flour
1½	cups sugar
1¼	teaspoons baking powder
1	teaspoon salt
½	cup vegetable oil
4	large egg yolks
¾	cup cold water
2	teaspoons vanilla extract
1	cup egg whites (from 7-8 large eggs)
½	teaspoon cream of tartar

Preheat oven to 350°F. Sift flour, sugar, baking powder and salt into a bowl. Make a well in center of flour mixture. Add oil, egg yolks, water and vanilla to the well. Mix for 1 minute with a stand mixer at low speed or a hand mixer at medium speed, scraping the bowl frequently. In a separate bowl, beat egg whites and cream of tartar with clean beaters to stiff (but not dry) peaks. Add beaten egg whites to batter ⅓ at a time. With a rubber spatula, fold 15 strokes after the first and second additions and 25 strokes after the third. Pour batter into an ungreased 10-inch tube cake pan. Bake for 55-65 minutes, or until a toothpick inserted in center comes out clean. Remove cake from oven and cool in inverted pan.

VARIATIONS:
- LEMON CHIFFON CAKE: Substitute 2 tablespoons strained lemon juice for 2 tablespoons of water. Omit vanilla. Add 1 tablespoon grated lemon zest.
- ORANGE CHIFFON CAKE: Substitute ¼ cup strained orange juice for ¼ cup of water. Omit vanilla. Add 1 tablespoon grated orange zest.
- PINEAPPLE CHIFFON CAKE: Substitute ¾ cup cold, unsweetened pineapple juice for the water

ALTITUDE ADJUSTMENTS:
6,500-8,500 feet: Same as 5,000 feet.
8,500+ feet: Decrease baking powder to 1 teaspoon in basic chiffon cake. Decrease baking powder to ¾ teaspoon in orange chiffon variation (lemon and pineapple chiffon variations use 1¼ teaspoons baking powder).

QUICK POUND CAKE
Makes One 10-inch Tube Cake

3	cups sifted cake flour or 2⅔ cups all-purpose flour
1¾	cups sugar
1	teaspoon baking powder
1	teaspoon salt
4	large eggs
¾	cup milk plus extra to mix with eggs
1½	sticks (¾ cup) butter or margarine
1	teaspoon grated lemon zest
1½	teaspoons vanilla extract

Preheat oven to 350°F. Sift together flour, sugar, baking powder and salt into a large bowl. Break eggs into a 1-cup measuring cup. Add enough milk to make 1 cup of liquid. Add egg mixture and butter to flour mixture. Beat for 3 minutes with an electric mixture at medium speed. Add ¾ cup of milk, lemon zest and vanilla. Beat for 2 minutes at medium speed. Pour batter into a greased and floured 10-inch tube cake pan. Bake for about 1 hour, or until a toothpick inserted in the center comes out clean. Remove from oven and cool upright completely before removing cake from pan.

*NOTE: This is a light, moist cake that is great served with fruits or sauces. It also makes an excellent base for strawberry shortcake!

WHITE CAKE
Makes Two 8-inch Layer Cakes

2¼ cups sifted cake flour
1¼ teaspoons baking powder
½ teaspoon salt
⅓ cup vegetable oil
½ cup milk
½ cup water
1 teaspoon vanilla extract
½ cup egg whites (from about 4 large eggs)
¼ teaspoon cream of tartar
1 cup sugar
White Frosting (recipe follows)

Preheat oven to 375°F. Grease and flour two 8-inch round cake pans. Mix and sift flour, baking powder and salt into a bowl. Add oil, milk, water and vanilla. Beat for 2 minutes with a mixer at medium speed, scraping the bowl frequently.

In a separate bowl, beat egg whites and cream of tartar with clean beaters until stiff (but not dry) peaks form. Gradually add sugar, beating until stiff (but not dry) peaks form. Fold egg white mixture into batter, using about 40 strokes. Pour batter into pans. Bake for about 27 minutes, or until a toothpick inserted in the center comes out clean. Remove cakes from oven and cool in pans for about 12 minutes. Remove cakes from pans and finish cooling on a wire rack. Frost cake, if desired.

ALTITUDE ADJUSTMENTS
6,500-8,500 feet: None.
8,500+ feet: Increase egg whites by 2 tablespoons (about 1 additional egg white.) Decrease sugar by 1 tablespoon.

WHITE FROSTING
1 stick (½ cup) butter, shortening or margarine
2½ tablespoons flour
¼ teaspoon salt
½ cup milk
½ teaspoon vanilla extract
3 cups powdered sugar, sifted

In a saucepan, melt butter. Remove from heat and blend in flour and salt. Slowly stir in milk. Return to stove and bring to a boil, stirring constantly. Boil for 1 minute. Remove from heat and stir in vanilla and powdered sugar. Place saucepan in a bowl of ice water and beat frosting until well blended and thick enough to spread.

YELLOW CAKE

Makes Two 9-inch Layer Cakes or Two 8x8-inch Cakes

3	cups sifted cake flour
2½	teaspoons baking powder
1	teaspoon salt
1	cup butter or shortening
1½	cups sugar
2	teaspoons vanilla extract
4	large egg yolks
1⅓	cups milk
4	large egg whites

Preheat oven to 375°F. Grease and flour two 9-inch round cake pans or two 8x8-inch baking pans. Mix and sift flour, baking powder and salt into a small bowl. In a large bowl, cream butter and sugar with mixer at medium speed until light and fluffy, about 5 minutes. Add vanilla and egg yolks; beat for 2 minutes at medium speed. Add flour mixture and milk alternately, ¼ at a time, mixing for 1 minute at low speed after each addition.

In a separate bowl, beat egg whites until stiff, about 75 strokes or 1 minute at low speed. Gently fold beaten egg whites into batter. Pour batter into pans. Bake for 25-30 minutes, or until a toothpick inserted in the center comes out clean. Remove cakes from oven and cool in pans for about 12 minutes. Remove cakes from pans and finish cooling on a wire rack.

ALTITUDE ADJUSTMENTS
6,500-8,500 feet: Decrease baking powder to 1⅞ teaspoons.
8,500+ feet: Decrease baking powder to 1⅛ teaspoons.

BANANA CAKE
Makes Two 9-inch Layer Cakes or One 9x13-inch Cake

A light, fine-textured cake with many frosting options.

2½	cups sifted cake flour
1⅓	cups sugar
¾	teaspoon baking powder
½	teaspoon baking soda
¼	teaspoon salt
½	cup vegetable oil
1	teaspoon almond extract
⅔	cup buttermilk, divided
3	large ripe bananas, mashed
2	large eggs
⅔	cup chopped walnuts (optional)

Preheat oven to 350°F. Grease and flour two 9-inch round cake pans or one 9x13-inch baking pan. Mix and sift cake flour, sugar, baking powder, baking soda and salt into a large bowl. Add oil, almond extract, ⅓ cup buttermilk and mashed bananas. Beat for 1 minute with a mixer at low speed. Add eggs and the remaining ⅓ cup of buttermilk; beat for 2 minutes at medium speed. Fold in chopped nuts, if desired. Pour batter into pans.

Bake for 35-45 minutes, or until a toothpick inserted in the center comes out clean. Remove cakes from oven and cool in pans for 10-12 minutes. Remove cakes from pans and finish cooling on a wire rack. Frost with coconut frosting (see page 29), cream cheese frosting (see page 38), white frosting (see page 26) or chocolate coconut frosting (see page 15).

OATMEAL CAKE
Makes One 9x9-inch Cake

1¼ cups quick-cooking oats
1⅓ cups boiling water
1   stick (½ cup) butter or margarine
1   cup packed brown sugar
1   teaspoon vanilla extract
3   large eggs
1½ cups sifted all-purpose flour
½   cup sugar
½   teaspoon salt
1   teaspoon baking soda
¾   teaspoon cinnamon
¼   teaspoon nutmeg
     Coconut frosting (recipe follows)

Put oats in a bowl. Pour boiling water over oats; cover and let stand for 20 minutes. Preheat oven to 350°F. Grease and flour the bottom of a 9x9-inch baking pan. Add butter, brown sugar, vanilla and eggs to oats; mix for 1 minute with a mixer at medium speed. In a separate bowl, mix and sift flour, sugar, salt, baking soda, cinnamon and nutmeg. Add flour mixture to oat mixture; mix for 1 minute at low speed. Pour batter into pan. Bake for about 60 minutes, or until a toothpick inserted in the center comes out clean. Frost hot cake, if desired. If frosting, turn oven to broil and broil frosted cake just until frosting is bubbly and lightly browned.

ALTITUDE ADJUSTMENTS
6,500-8,500 feet: None.
8,500+ feet: None.

COCONUT FROSTING
½   stick (¼ cup) margarine
½   cup packed brown sugar
3   tablespoons cream (or undiluted evaporated milk)
⅓   cup chopped walnuts
¾   cup shredded coconut

Mix together margarine, brown sugar and cream. Add nuts and coconut; mix well.

BURNT SUGAR CAKE
Makes Two 9-inch Layer Cakes, One 9x13-inch Cake or 24 Cupcakes

2½	cups sifted cake flour
1⅞	teaspoons baking powder
½	teaspoon salt
1½	cups sugar
⅓	cup butter or shortening
2	large eggs
1	teaspoon vanilla extract
1	cup milk
3	tablespoons burnt sugar syrup (recipe follows)
	Burnt sugar frosting (recipe follows)

Preheat oven to 375°F. Grease and flour two 9-inch cake pans, one 9x13-inch baking pan or muffin cups. Mix and sift flour, baking powder, salt and sugar into a bowl. Add butter, eggs, vanilla, milk and burnt sugar syrup. Beat for 30 seconds with a mixer at low speed, scraping the bowl frequently. Beat for 4½ minutes more at high speed, scraping the bowl 4-5 times. Pour batter into pans. Bake for the time recommended below, or until a toothpick inserted in the center comes out clean.* Remove cakes from oven and cool in pans for 12 minutes. Remove cakes from pans and finish cooling on a wire rack. Frost with burnt sugar frosting, if desired. Serve with ice cream.

*Two 9-inch layer cakes: 28-30 minutes. One 9x13-inch cake: 30-35 minutes. 24 cupcakes (½ full): about 25 minutes.

ALTITUDE ADJUSTMENTS:
6,500-8,500 feet: Decrease baking powder to 1¼ teaspoons.
8,500+ feet: Decrease baking powder to ⅞ teaspoon. Decrease sugar to 1¼ cups.

BURNT SUGAR SYRUP
½	cup sugar
½	cup boiling water

In a heavy skillet, stir sugar over low heat until melted and well browned. Add boiling water and cook, stirring, until smooth. Cool before using. Use leftover syrup in burnt sugar frosting or store, covered, in the refrigerator.

BURNT SUGAR FROSTING

1	stick (½ cup) butter
2½	tablespoons flour
¼	teaspoon salt
2	tablespoons burnt sugar syrup (above)
6	tablespoons milk
½	teaspoon vanilla extract
3	cups powdered sugar, sifted

In a saucepan, melt butter (if desired, brown the butter over low heat for more flavor). Remove from heat and stir in flour and salt. Slowly stir in burnt sugar syrup and milk. Return to stove and bring to a boil, stirring constantly. Boil for 1 minute. Remove from heat, stir in vanilla and powdered sugar. Place pan in bowl of ice water and beat frosting until well blended and thick enough to spread.

WHOLE WHEAT CARROT CAKE
Makes One Bundt Cake

¾	cup vegetable oil
1½	cups sugar
4	large eggs
½	cup milk
2	cups shredded carrots
1	(8-ounce) can crushed pineapple, undrained
2½	cups whole-wheat flour
2	teaspoons cinnamon
1	teaspoon baking soda
½	teaspoon salt
½	cup raisins
	Cream cheese frosting (see page 38)

Preheat oven to 350°F. Grease bottom and sides of a Bundt cake pan. In a large bowl, combine vegetable oil, sugar, eggs, milk, carrots and undrained pineapple. In a separate bowl, combine whole-wheat flour, cinnamon, baking soda and salt. Add flour mixture to carrot mixture; mix until well blended. Stir in raisins. Pour batter into pan. Bake for 40-45 minutes, or until toothpick inserted in the center comes out clean. Remove cake from oven and cool in pan for 30 minutes. Remove cake from pan. Frost cooled cake with cream cheese frosting, if desired.

DARK FRUIT CAKE
Makes Five 7 ½ x 3 ¾ - inch Cakes

½	pound pitted dates, diced
½	pound candied pineapple, diced
¾	pound diced candied citron*
¼	pound diced candied orange peel
¾	pound diced candied lemon peel
½	pound currants
½	pound raisins
½	pound candied cherries, whole or halved
½	pound almonds, blanched and slivered
½	pound pecan halves
1	cup + 2 cups all-purpose flour
1½	teaspoons cinnamon
1	teaspoon nutmeg
½	teaspoon allspice
½	teaspoon salt
1	stick (½ cup) butter or ½ cup shortening
½	cup packed dark brown sugar
8	large egg whites
½	cup orange juice
½	cup honey, warmed slightly
	Glaze (recipe follows)
	Rum, brandy or other liqueur (optional)

Preheat oven to 275°F. Grease five 7½x3¾-inch loaf pans and line with paper (waxed, brown or parchment). Cut paper to fit bottoms of pans and to extend ¼-inch above sides of pans. Fit papers into pans and grease papers. Cut 5 more papers to fit over tops of pans and grease on one side.

Put fruits and nuts in a large bowl. Add 1 cup flour and mix until all pieces are evenly coated. Sift together the remaining 2 cups of flour, cinnamon, nutmeg, allspice and salt into a bowl. In a separate bowl, cream butter until light. Gradually add sugar to butter; cream until light and fluffy. Add egg whites; mix thoroughly.

Combine orange juice and honey in a small bowl. Beat flour mixture and orange juice mixture alternately, ⅓ at a time, into butter mixture, mixing well after each addition. Pour batter over fruit and nuts; blend thoroughly to evenly distribute fruit and nuts. Pack mixture to within ¾-inch of tops of pans, rounding mixture slightly on top. Cover tops of pans with papers, greased side toward batter.

Bake for about 2½ hours, or until a toothpick inserted in the center comes out clean. If cakes need to brown more, lift papers from the tops of the pans during the last few minutes of baking. Remove cakes from oven and cool in pans on wire racks for 20 minutes. Remove cakes from pans and carefully remove papers. When completely cool, brush cakes with hot glaze, if desired. Immediately decorate with fruit and nuts. Return glaze mixture to a boil and again brush hot glaze over cakes. Let the glaze dry before wrapping the cakes for storage.

When completely cool, the cakes may be wrapped first in waxed paper, then in aluminum foil. If preferred, the cakes may be wrapped in cheese cloth soaked in brandy or wine, then wrapped in foil. Store cakes in a cool place for at least 1 week before serving. When slicing cakes, use a very sharp knife to avoid tearing the fruit and nuts.

*Citron is a special citrus fruit grown for its thick skin. Candied citron is available in most groceries and specialty food stores.

ALTITUDE ADJUSTMENTS:
6,500-8,500 feet: Increase egg whites to 10.
8,500+ feet: Increase egg whites to 10.

GLAZE
½   cup orange juice
½   cup light corn syrup

Bring orange juice and syrup to a rolling boil; remove from heat. Use hot.

APPLESAUCE CAKE
Makes One 9x9-inch Cake or 24 Cupcakes

1	tablespoon + 1 cup sifted all-purpose flour
½	cup walnuts (optional)
1	cup raisins
1	cup whole-wheat flour
½	teaspoon cinnamon
¼	teaspoon nutmeg
½	teaspoon ground cloves
1	teaspoon baking soda
½	teaspoon baking powder
½	teaspoon salt
⅔	cup sugar
½	cup vegetable oil
1¼	cups applesauce
2	large eggs

Preheat oven to 350°F. Grease and flour a 9x9-inch baking pan or line muffin cups with paper liners. Add 1 tablespoon flour to nuts and raisins; stir until well coated. Mix and sift whole-wheat flour, the remaining 1 cup all-purpose flour, cinnamon, nutmeg, cloves, baking soda, baking powder, salt and sugar into a bowl. Add oil, applesauce and eggs; beat for 30 seconds with a mixer at low speed, scraping the bowl frequently. Beat for 3½ minutes more at medium speed, scraping the bowl 3-4 times. Stir in flour-coated raisins and nuts. Pour batter into pans. Bake for time recommended below, or until a toothpick inserted in the center comes out clean.* Remove cake from oven and immediately loosen cake from pan by running a thin spatula or knife around the edges. Turn cake out onto a wire rack to cool. Wrap cooled cake to prevent drying.

*One 9x9-inch cake: 35-40 minutes. 24 cupcakes: 20-23 minutes.

NOTE: If a larger cake is desired, increase all ingredients by ½ and bake in a 9x13-inch baking pan for about 50 minutes.

ALTITUDE ADJUSTMENTS:
6,500-8,500 feet: Omit baking powder. Raise oven temperature to 375°F.
8,500+ feet: Omit baking powder. Raise oven temperature to 375°F.

WARM APPLE TORTE
Makes One 9-inch Torte

This torte is delicious served with warm caramel sauce or apple butter and whipped cream or ice cream.

¾	stick (6 tablespoons) butter, softened
1	cup sugar
1½	teaspoons grated lemon zest
¾	teaspoon cinnamon
¼	teaspoon salt
1	large egg
¼	teaspoon baking soda
6	tablespoons milk
1	cup all-purpose flour, divided
½	teaspoon baking powder
⅜	pound Granny Smith apples, peeled, cored and grated

Preheat oven to 350°F. Butter and flour a 9-inch round cake pan. With a mixer at medium speed, cream butter, sugar, lemon zest, cinnamon and salt until light and fluffy. Add egg; beat well. Dissolve baking soda in milk; mix ½ of this mixture into the butter mixture. Add ½ cup of flour and baking powder to the butter mixture; mix well. Blend in remaining milk mixture, then the remaining ½ cup of flour. Fold in the apples. Pour batter into pan. Bake for 30-35 minutes, or until a toothpick inserted in the center comes out clean. Serve warm.

—Recipe courtesy of Melissa Craven

RASPBERRY WALNUT TORTE

Makes One 9x13-inch Torte

1	stick (½ cup) butter, softened
½	cup powdered sugar
1	cup + ¼ cup all-purpose flour
1	(10-ounce) package frozen raspberries, thawed (juice reserved)
¾	cup chopped walnuts
2	large eggs
1	cup white sugar
½	teaspoon salt
½	teaspoon baking powder
1	teaspoon vanilla extract
	Raspberry sauce (recipe follows)

Preheat oven to 350°F. Grease a 9x13-inch baking pan. Cream butter, 1 cup of flour and powdered sugar. Press this mixture into the bottom of the pan. Bake for 15 minutes, then cool.

Drain the raspberries, reserving the juice for the raspberry sauce. Spoon the berries over the crust. Sprinkle the nuts over the berries. Beat the eggs and white sugar until light and fluffy. Add the salt, baking powder, vanilla and the remaining ¼ cup of flour. Blend well and pour over the nuts. Bake for 30-35 minutes, or until golden brown. Cut the torte into squares and serve with the raspberry sauce.

RASPBERRY SAUCE

	Raspberry juice reserved from thawed raspberries (above)
½	cup water
2	tablespoons cornstarch
½	cup sugar
1	tablespoon fresh lemon juice

Combine reserved raspberry juice, water, cornstarch and sugar in a saucepan. Bring to a boil, lower the heat and simmer until thickened and clear. Stir in the lemon juice and cool.

—Recipe courtesy of Melissa Craven

HOLIDAY CRANBERRY CAKE
Makes One 8x8-inch Cake

1	large egg, beaten
½	cup + 2 tablespoons sugar
½	cup milk
2	tablespoons vegetable oil
2	tablespoons orange juice
1	teaspoon grated orange zest
¼	teaspoon almond extract
1	cup all-purpose flour
1½	teaspoons baking powder
½	teaspoon salt
8	ounces (2 cups) fresh cranberries
	Streusel topping (recipe follows)

Preheat oven to 375°F. Grease an 8x8-inch baking pan. Combine egg, ½ cup sugar, milk, oil, orange juice, orange zest and almond extract in a large bowl; mix thoroughly. Combine flour, baking powder and salt in a medium bowl; mix into egg mixture. Pour into pan.

Toss cranberries and the remaining 2 tablespoons sugar; spoon over batter. Sprinkle streusel topping over cranberries. Bake for 25-30 minutes, or until a toothpick inserted in the center comes out clean. Serve warm.

STREUSEL TOPPING

½	cup packed brown sugar
⅓	cup all-purpose flour
1	teaspoon cinnamon
2	tablespoons butter, melted
½	cup finely chopped walnuts (optional)

Mix streusel ingredients together with a fork.

—Recipe courtesy of the Wheat Foods Council

CHOCOLATE CARROT CAKE
Makes One 9x13-inch Cake

2   cups flour
1½   cups sugar
1   cup vegetable oil
½   cup orange juice
¼   cup unsweetened cocoa powder
2   teaspoons baking soda
1   teaspoon salt
1   teaspoon cinnamon
1   teaspoon vanilla extract
4   large eggs
2   cups shredded carrots
1   (3.5-ounce) package (1⅓ cups) shredded coconut
     Cream cheese frosting (recipe follows)

Preheat oven to 350°F. Grease and flour a 9x13-inch baking pan. In a large bowl, with a mixer at low speed, mix all of the ingredients, except carrots and coconut, until well blended, scraping the bowl often. Mix at high speed for 2 minutes more. Stir in carrots and coconut. Spoon batter into pan. Bake for 35-45 minutes, or until a toothpick inserted in the center comes out clean. Remove cake from oven and cool on a wire rack. Frost with cream cheese frosting, if desired. Store in the refrigerator.

CREAM CHEESE FROSTING
1   (8-ounce) package cream cheese, chilled
½   stick (¼ cup) butter, softened
1   teaspoon vanilla extract
½   teaspoon almond extract (or use 1 more teaspoon vanilla extract)
2   cups powdered sugar

Beat together cream cheese, butter, vanilla extract and almond extract with a mixer at medium speed until combined (do not overbeat). Gradually add powdered sugar, beating at low speed until smooth (do not overbeat).

—Recipe courtesy of Ambiance Inn, *Colorado Bed & Breakfast Cookbook*

CARROT CAKE
Makes 1 Bundt Cake

¾   cup vegetable oil
1¼   cups sugar
4   large eggs
½   cup milk
2   teaspoons vanilla extract
2   cups shredded carrot
1   (8-ounce) can crushed pineapple, undrained
2½   cups all-purpose flour
2   teaspoons cinnamon
1   teaspoon baking soda
½   teaspoon salt
½   cup raisins
     Cream cheese frosting (see page 38)

Preheat oven to 350°F. Grease the bottom and sides of a Bundt cake pan. In a large bowl, combine oil, sugar, eggs, milk, vanilla, carrot and undrained pineapple. In a separate bowl, mix and sift flour, cinnamon, baking soda and salt. Add flour mixture to carrot mixture; stir until well blended. Stir in the raisins. Pour batter into pan. Bake for 40-45 minutes, or until a toothpick inserted in the center comes out clean. Remove from oven and cool in pan for 30 minutes. Remove cake from pan and frost with cream cheese frosting, if desired.

VARIATION: For a healthier cake, decrease oil to ½ cup; decrease sugar to 1 cup; omit 2 of the eggs; and substitute whole-wheat flour for the all-purpose flour. Decrease baking time to 30-40 minutes, or until a toothpick inserted in the center comes out clean.

ALTITUDE ADJUSTMENTS:
6,500-8,500 feet: None.
8,500+ feet: None.

CHOCOLATE ZUCCHINI CAKE
Makes One 9x13-inch Cake

A wonderfully moist cake that is a perfect way to use up that extra zucchini. This cake is good on the first day, but the next day... it's better!

½	cup buttermilk or sour milk*
1	teaspoon baking soda
1	stick (½ cup) butter or margarine, softened
1	teaspoon salt
1¾	cups sugar
1	teaspoon vanilla extract
½	cup vegetable oil
2	large eggs
2½	cups flour
1½	teaspoons baking powder
¼	cup unsweetened cocoa powder
2	cups grated zucchini
1	cup chopped walnuts
1	cup chocolate chips (optional)

Preheat oven to 350°F. Grease a 9x13-inch baking pan. In a small bowl, combine buttermilk and baking soda; stir until baking soda has dissolved. In a separate bowl, mix butter, salt, sugar, vanilla, oil and eggs. Add buttermilk mixture; mix well.

In another bowl, mix flour, baking powder, cocoa, zucchini and walnuts; add to the egg mixture and mix well. Pour batter into pan. Bake for 40-50 minutes, or until a toothpick inserted in the center comes out clean.

If desired, at the end of the baking, sprinkle the cake with chocolate chips and continue baking until the chips are just melted to "frost" the cake.

*NOTE: To make sour milk, mix ½ cup milk with 1½ teaspoons lemon juice or vinegar; let stand for 5 minutes.

—Recipe courtesy of Dona Erickson, Front Range Organic Gardeners,
Colorado Farmers' Market Cookbook

PINEAPPLE SHEET CAKE
Makes One 9x13-inch Cake

This is a delicious, moist cake with a terrific, subtle pineapple flavor.

2	cups all-purpose flour
1	cup sugar
1	teaspoon baking soda
1	teaspoon salt
1	(15-ounce) can crushed pineapple, undrained
2	large eggs
½	cup vegetable oil
1	teaspoon vanilla extract
	Coconut nut topping (optional – recipe follows)

Preheat oven to 350°F. Grease the bottom of an 9x13-inch baking pan. Stir flour, sugar, baking soda and salt together. Add undrained pineapple, eggs, oil and vanilla; mix well. Pour batter into pan. Bake for 20-25 minutes, or until a toothpick inserted in the center comes out clean. Remove cake from oven. Top hot cake with coconut-nut topping, if desired. Slice and serve from pan.

COCONUT NUT TOPPING

1	cup sugar
½	stick (¼ cup) butter or margarine
⅔	cup evaporated milk
1	cup shredded coconut
1	cup chopped walnuts
1	teaspoon vanilla extract

Combine sugar, butter and evaporated milk in a saucepan. Cook over medium-low heat, stirring constantly, until slightly thickened, about 10 minutes. Remove from heat. Stir in coconut, nuts and vanilla.

COOKIES,
BAR COOKIES
& BISCOTTI

CONEJOS COOKIES
Makes 6 Dozen Cookies

1	cup (2 sticks) butter, softened
1	cup white sugar
1	cup packed brown sugar
1	large egg
1	cup vegetable oil
1	tablespoon vanilla extract
1	cup old-fashioned rolled oats
1	cup crisp rice cereal (such as Rice Krispies)
½	cup shredded coconut
½	cup chopped toasted pecans
3½	cups all-purpose flour
1	teaspoon salt
1	teaspoon baking soda

Preheat oven to 325°F. In a large bowl, cream together butter, white sugar and brown sugar until light and fluffy. Add egg, oil and vanilla; mix well. Add oats, crispy rice cereal, coconut and pecans; stir well. Sift together flour, salt and baking soda into a medium bowl; stir into the batter until well blended. Drop dough by teaspoonsful onto a greased, insulated baking sheet (insulated baking sheets help keep cookies from browning too much on the bottom). Bake for about 15 minutes.

—Recipe courtesy of the Conejos Ranch,
Colorado Bed & Breakfast Cookbook

MOCHA CHIP COOKIES
Makes 8 Dozen Small Cookies

1	cup + 1½ cups semi-sweet chocolate chips
2	sticks (1 cup) butter, softened
1	cup packed brown sugar
1	cup white sugar
2	large eggs
4	tablespoons instant coffee granules
4	teaspoons hot water
2	teaspoons vanilla extract
3	cups all-purpose flour
1½	teaspoons baking soda
½	teaspoon salt

Melt 1 cup of chocolate chips over low heat; set aside. In a large bowl, cream together butter, brown sugar and white sugar. Add the eggs; mix until smooth. Stir coffee granules into the hot water until dissolved; stir into the butter mixture. Stir in the vanilla. Mix in the melted chocolate.

In small bowl, combine flour, baking soda and salt; mix gradually into the butter mixture. Stir in the remaining 1½ cups of chocolate chips. Refrigerate dough until stiff.

Preheat oven to 350°F. Form chilled dough into small balls. Place on an ungreased baking sheet and bake for 8-10 minutes. Remove from oven when surface looks "cracked" and dough has spread somewhat, but is not yet flat.

—Recipe courtesy of Boulder Victoria,
Colorado Bed & Breakfast Cookbook

BANANA CHOCOLATE CHIP COOKIES

Makes About 3 Dozen Cookies

1½	cups flour
2	teaspoons baking powder
1	teaspoon salt
1	stick (½ cup) butter, softened
⅔	cup white sugar
⅔	cup packed dark brown sugar
1½	teaspoons vanilla extract
1-1½	ripe bananas
2	large eggs
½	cup old-fashioned rolled oats
1½	cups wheat germ
1	(12-ounce) package (2 cups) semisweet chocolate chips
1	cup walnuts (optional)

Preheat oven to 350°F. Sift together flour, baking powder and salt into a medium bowl; set aside. In a large bowl, cream the butter with a mixer at low speed. Beat in white sugar, brown sugar, vanilla and banana. Add the eggs; beat well. Beat the flour mixture into the butter mixture, just until blended. Add oats and wheat germ; mix until blended. Stir in chocolate chips and walnuts by hand.

Roll the dough into balls using about 1 heaping tablespoon of dough per cookie. Place the cookies on 2 greased baking sheets, allowing plenty of room for the dough to spread while baking (the cookies will be about 4½ inches in diameter). Using a wet fork, flatten the cookies to a ½-inch thickness. Put both baking sheets in the oven and bake for 18-20 minutes, or until cookies are light brown and the tops spring back when pressed. Remove cookies from oven and cool for 5 minutes on the baking sheets, then transfer to wire racks to finish cooling. Store cooled cookies in an airtight container.

—Recipe courtesy of Melissa Craven

CHOCOLATE CHOCOLATE CHIP COOKIES

Makes about 2 Dozen Cookies

2	sticks (1 cup) butter
1	cup white sugar
½	cup packed brown sugar
1	large egg
1	teaspoon vanilla extract
1¾	cups + 2 tablespoons all-purpose flour
1	teaspoon baking soda
⅔	cup unsweetened cocoa powder
2	tablespoons milk
1	cup chopped pecans or walnuts
1½	cups chocolate chips

Preheat oven to 375°F. Cream butter, white sugar and brown sugar together. Stir in egg and vanilla. Mix in flour, baking soda, cocoa and milk. Stir in the nuts and chocolate chips. Drop dough by tablespoonsful, spaced well apart, on a greased baking sheet. Bake for 10-15 minutes.

—Recipe courtesy of Melissa Craven

BASIC DROP COOKIES WITH SEVEN VARIATIONS

Makes 5 to 6 Dozen Cookies

An easy drop cookie with seven variations!

½	cup white sugar
½	cup packed brown sugar
⅔	cup butter or shortening, softened, or ½ cup vegetable oil
2	large eggs
1	teaspoon vanilla extract
2	cups all-purpose flour
1	teaspoon salt
1	teaspoon baking powder

Preheat oven to 375°F. In a large bowl, cream white sugar, brown sugar and butter. Add eggs and vanilla; beat until smooth. In a separate bowl, combine flour, salt and baking powder; add to sugar mixture, a little at a time, mixing thoroughly after each addition. Drop by slightly rounded teaspoonsful, 1½ inches apart, onto an ungreased baking sheet. Bake for 10-12 minutes, or until lightly browned. Remove cookies from baking sheet immediately and cool on a wire rack.

VARIATIONS:
- APPLE SPICE COOKIES: Add 1 teaspoon nutmeg and 1 teaspoon cinnamon to flour mixture. Stir 1 cup finely chopped peeled apple into dough.
- BANANA NUT COOKIES: Stir 1 cup mashed banana and ½ cup chopped nuts into dough.
- CARROT COOKIES: Add 1 cup grated raw carrots and 4 teaspoons grated orange zest with eggs and vanilla.
- CHOCOLATE CHIP COOKIES: Stir 1 cup chocolate chips and 2 tablespoons water into dough.
- HONEY SPICE COOKIES: Omit brown sugar and vanilla. Add ⅓ cup honey with the eggs. Add to flour mixture ½ teaspoon each: cinnamon, nutmeg, allspice and ground cloves.
- MARASCHINO CHERRY NUT COOKIES: Stir ½ cup chopped, drained maraschino cherries and ½ cup chopped nuts into dough.
- PINEAPPLE RAISIN COOKIES: Stir ½ cup drained crushed pineapple and ½ cup golden raisins into dough.

CARROT RAISIN COOKIES
Makes 4 dozen (2-inch) Cookies

A nutritious treat.

⅓	cup butter or shortening, softened
⅓	cup packed brown sugar
¼	cup molasses
1	large egg
¼	cup water or milk
1	cup all-purpose flour
¼	cup non-fat dry milk
½	teaspoon ground cloves
1	teaspoon cinnamon
½	teaspoon salt
¼	teaspoon baking soda
1½	cups quick-cooking oats
1	cup grated carrot
½	cup raisins
1	teaspoon grated lemon zest (optional)

Preheat oven to 375°F. In a large bowl, beat together butter, sugar, molasses, egg and water or milk. In a separate bowl, combine flour, dry milk, cloves, cinnamon, salt, baking soda and oats. Add flour mixture to butter mixture, a little at a time, mixing thoroughly after each addition. Add grated carrot, raisins and lemon zest; stir until well mixed. Drop dough by teaspoonsful, 1 ½ inches apart, onto a lightly greased baking sheet. Bake for 10-15 minutes, or until lightly browned. Remove cookies from baking sheet immediately and cool on a wire rack.

OATMEAL COOKIES
Makes 5 to 6 Dozen Cookies

A crisp cookie with softer banana and pumpkin variations.

⅔	cup butter or shortening, softened
⅓	cup white sugar
⅔	cup packed brown sugar
2	large eggs
1	teaspoon vanilla extract
1⅓	cups all-purpose flour
¼	cup non-fat dry milk
½	teaspoon baking soda
½	teaspoon salt
½	teaspoon nutmeg
1	teaspoon cinnamon
2	cups quick-cooking oats
½	cup chopped walnuts (optional)
½	cup raisins, chocolate chips or Craisins (optional)

Preheat oven to 375°F. In a large bowl, cream butter, white sugar and brown sugar. Beat in egg and vanilla. In a separate bowl, combine flour, dry milk, baking soda, salt, nutmeg and cinnamon. Add flour mixture to butter mixture, a little at a time, mixing thoroughly after each addition. Stir in oats, nuts and raisins, chocolate chips or Craisins. Drop by teaspoonsful, 1½ inches apart, onto an ungreased baking sheet. Bake for 12-15 minutes. Remove cookies from baking sheet immediately and cool on a wire rack.

VARIATIONS:
- PUMPKIN OATMEAL COOKIES: Increase white sugar to ½ cup. Add 1 cup cooked or canned pumpkin purée with eggs and vanilla. Mix ¼ teaspoon ground cloves and ¼ teaspoon ground ginger into flour mixture.
- BANANA OATMEAL COOKIES: Add 1 cup mashed banana with egg and vanilla.
- OATMEAL CHOCOLATE CHIP COOKIES: Add 1 cup chocolate chips with the nuts and raisins.

ZUCCHINI COOKIES
Makes 4 Dozen (2-inch) Cookies

Another way to use this prolific vegetable.

1	cup grated unpeeled zucchini
¾	cup sugar
1	stick (½ cup) butter or shortening, softened, or vegetable oil
1	large egg, beaten
1	teaspoon vanilla extract
1	cup all-purpose flour
1	cup whole-wheat flour
1	teaspoon baking soda
½	teaspoon salt
½	teaspoon nutmeg
½	teaspoon ground cloves
1	teaspoon cinnamon
1	cup raisins
½	cup chopped walnuts (optional)

Preheat oven to 375°F. Beat grated zucchini, sugar, butter, egg and vanilla together in a large bowl. In a separate bowl, sift or stir together all-purpose flour, whole-wheat flour, baking soda, salt, nutmeg, cloves and cinnamon. Add flour mixture to zucchini mixture; mix thoroughly. Stir in raisins and nuts. Drop by teaspoonsful, 1½ inches apart, onto a greased baking sheet. Bake for 12-15 minutes. Remove cookies to a wire rack to cool.

DECADENT CHOCOLATE SHORTBREAD BARS
Makes 32 (2-inch) Bars

1¼ cups flour
¼ cup sugar
1 stick (½ cup) + 2 tablespoons butter, softened
  Filling (recipe follows)

Preheat oven to 300°F. Grease a rimmed baking sheet. Combine flour and sugar. Rub the butter into the flour mixture. Knead into a ball. Press into the bottom of the baking sheet. Bake for 15-20 minutes, or until golden.

FILLING
1 stick (½ cup) butter
½ cup + 2 tablespoons packed brown sugar
¼ cup dark corn syrup
1 (14-ounce) can sweetened condensed milk
½ teaspoon vanilla extract
¼ pound best quality semi-sweet or dark chocolate

Put butter, brown sugar, corn syrup and condensed milk into a saucepan over low heat. Cook, stirring, until sugar is dissolved. Bring to a simmer over medium heat. Simmer, stirring, for 7 minutes (be careful not to scorch the mixture). Add vanilla and stir well. Pour the filling over the shortbread. Allow to cool. Melt the chocolate and spread over the filling. When cool, cut into 2-inch squares.

—Recipe courtesy of Melissa Craven

TRAIL BARS
Makes 36 bars

These bars make great hiking snacks.

1¾	cups whole-wheat flour
½	cup sugar
½	cup non-fat dry milk
¼	cup wheat germ
1	teaspoon baking powder
¾	teaspoon salt
½	cup vegetable oil
2	large eggs
¼	cup honey
¼	cup molasses
1	cup raisins
¾	cup chopped dried fruit (such as apricots, cherries, dates, etc.)
½	cup sunflower seeds

Preheat oven to 350°F. Grease the bottom of a 9x13-inch baking pan. Mix whole-wheat flour, sugar, dry milk, wheat germ, baking powder and salt. Add oil, eggs, honey and molasses; mix until well blended. Stir in raisins, dried fruit and sunflower seeds. Pour batter into pan. Bake for 30-40 minutes, or until a toothpick inserted in the center comes out clean. Remove from oven and cool in pan. Cut into bars and remove from pan.

APPLE RAISIN BARS
Makes 36 Bars

A quick bar cookie with a soft, cake-like texture and three variations.

¾	cup sugar
⅓	cup vegetable oil or 1 stick (½ cup butter), softened
2	large eggs
3	tablespoons milk
1½	teaspoons vanilla extract
1⅔	cups all-purpose flour
½	teaspoon baking soda
¾	teaspoon salt
1	teaspoon cinnamon
¾	cup chopped peeled apples
¾	cup raisins or Craisins
⅓	cup chopped walnuts (optional)
	Spice frosting (recipe follows)

Preheat oven to 375°F. Grease the bottom of a 9x13-inch baking pan. In a large bowl, combine sugar, oil or butter, eggs, milk and vanilla. In a separate bowl, combine flour, baking soda, salt and cinnamon; add to sugar mixture and stir until blended. Stir in apples, raisins and nuts. Spread batter into pan. Bake for 15-20 minutes, or until top springs back when touched lightly in the center. Remove from oven. Cool slightly. Frost with spice frosting. Cut into bars and remove from pan.

SPICE FROSTING

¼	cup packed brown sugar
3	tablespoons butter or margarine
2	tablespoons milk
½	teaspoon cinnamon
¼	teaspoon ground ginger
¼	teaspoon ground cloves
1	teaspoon vanilla extract
1	cup powdered sugar, sifted

Combine brown sugar, butter, milk, cinnamon, ginger and cloves in a saucepan.

Cook over medium-low heat, stirring constantly, until mixture bubbles. Remove from heat; stir in vanilla. Slowly beat in powdered sugar until mixture is a spreading consistency.

VARIATIONS:
- SPICY PUMPKIN BARS: Omit milk, apples and raisins. Add 1 cup cooked or canned pumpkin purée. Mix ½ teaspoon ground cloves and ¼ teaspoon ground ginger into dry ingredients.
- DOUBLE CHOCOLATE CAKE BROWNIES: Decrease flour to 1⅓ cups. Mix ⅓ cup unsweetened cocoa powder into dry ingredients. Substitute ¾ cup chocolate chips for the chopped apples and raisins. Omit cinnamon, if desired.
- GRANOLA BAR COOKIES: Decrease sugar to ½ cup. Add 6 tablespoons orange juice. Omit the milk. Add ½ teaspoon almond extract with the vanilla extract. Substitute ¾ cup granola for the chopped apple.

APPLESAUCE DREAM BARS
Makes 36 bars

1	stick (½ cup) butter or margarine, softened
½	cup packed brown sugar
1¼	cups all-purpose flour
½	cup non-fat dry milk
1	teaspoon cinnamon
½	teaspoon salt
½	teaspoon baking soda
1½	cups quick-cooking oats
1½	cups applesauce

Preheat oven to 375°F. Grease a 9x13-inch baking pan. Beat together butter and sugar until light and fluffy. In a separate bowl, combine flour, dry milk, cinnamon, salt and baking soda. Stir in oats. Mix flour mixture into butter mixture to make a fine crumb. Press ½ of crumb mixture into the bottom of the pan. Spread with applesauce. Sprinkle with remaining crumb mixture and press firmly. Bake for about 30 minutes, or until golden brown. Cool, then cut into bars. Store in the refrigerator.

HONEY ALMOND BISCOTTI

Makes about 2 Dozen Biscotti

2	cups all-purpose flour
¾	cup sugar
¾	cup whole blanched almonds
¾	cup finely ground unblanched almonds
2	teaspoons baking soda
1½	teaspoons baking powder
2	teaspoons salt
2	teaspoons cinnamon
⅓	cup honey, warmed slightly
2	eggs
⅓	cup water
1	tablespoon almond extract or 4 teaspoons almond paste

Preheat oven to 350°F. Grease a baking sheet. In a medium bowl, mix flour, sugar, whole almonds, finely ground almonds, baking soda, baking powder, salt and cinnamon. In a separate bowl, combine honey, eggs, water and almond extract; add to flour mixture and mix until well blended. Put dough on a lightly floured surface. Divide dough in half. Form each half into a 2x12-inch log. Put logs on baking sheet. Bake for 30 minutes. Remove from oven and cool for 10 minutes.

Put logs on a cutting board. With a serrated knife, using a sawing motion, cut each log diagonally into ½-inch slices. Put slices, cut-side-up, on the baking sheet. Bake for 10 minutes. Turn slices and bake for 10-12 minutes more, or until golden brown (centers will be slightly soft, but will harden as they cool). Remove from oven and put biscotti on a wire rack to cool.

—Recipe courtesy of the Wheat Foods Council

CHOCOLATE CHIP BISCOTTI

Makes about 2 Dozen Biscotti

2	cups all-purpose flour
⅔	cup sugar
1	teaspoon baking soda
½	teaspoon salt
1	cup semi-sweet chocolate chips
3	large eggs, beaten
2	tablespoons milk
1	teaspoon vanilla extract

Preheat oven to 350°F. Grease a baking sheet. In a medium bowl, mix flour, sugar, baking soda, salt and chocolate chips. Add eggs, milk and vanilla; stir until blended. Put dough on a lightly floured surface. Knead 8-10 times. Form dough into a 2x16-inch log. Put log on baking sheet. Bake for 30 minutes. Remove from oven and cool for 10 minutes.

Put log on a cutting board. With a serrated knife, using a sawing motion, cut log diagonally into ½-inch slices. Put slices, cut-side-up, on the baking sheet. Bake for 10 minutes. Turn slices and bake for 10-12 minutes more, or until golden brown (centers will be slightly soft, but will harden as they cool). Remove from oven and put biscotti on a wire rack to cool.

—Recipe courtesy of the Wheat Foods Council

QUICK BREADS, COFFEE CAKES & MUFFINS

MEGAN MILLER'S SCRUMPTIOUS PUMPKIN BREAD
Makes 1 Loaf

1¼	cups cooked or canned pumpkin purée
⅓	cup water
2	large eggs
½	cup vegetable oil
1½	cups sugar
½	teaspoon nutmeg
2	teaspoons cinnamon
¾	teaspoon salt
1	teaspoon baking soda
1¾	cups flour
½	cup chopped walnuts (optional)

Preheat oven to 350°F. Grease a 9x5-inch loaf pan. In a large bowl, combine pumpkin, water, eggs, oil and sugar; mix well. Add remaining ingredients; mix until smooth and well combined. Pour into pan. Bake for 60-65 minutes, or until a toothpick inserted in the center comes out clean.

—Recipe courtesy of Megan Miller, Rock Creek Farm

WHOLE WHEAT QUICK BREAD
Makes 1 Loaf

A coarse-textured, rib-sticking quick bread with a choice of fruit flavors.

¼	cup oil or shortening
½	cup sugar
1	large egg
1	cup applesauce
1½	cups all-purpose flour
1½	cups whole-wheat flour
½	teaspoon salt
1	teaspoon baking soda
1	cup buttermilk
½	cup chopped nuts

Preheat oven to 350°F. Grease the bottom of a 9x5-inch loaf pan. In a large bowl, cream together oil or shortening and sugar. Beat in egg. Stir in applesauce. In a separate bowl, sift or stir together all-purpose flour, whole-wheat flour, salt and baking soda. Add flour mixture and buttermilk alternately to sugar mixture, ⅓ at a time, stirring after each addition. Fold in chopped nuts. Pour batter into pan. Bake for about 75 minutes, or until a toothpick inserted in the center comes out clean. Remove bread from oven and cool in pan.

VARIATION: Substitute ¼ cup apple juice and ¾ cup of grated peeled apple or unsweetened cooked, mashed prunes, apricots or cranberries for the applesauce.

ZUCCHINI CARROT BREAD
Makes 1 Loaf

A healthy, tasty whole-wheat quick bread with fresh zucchini and carrots.

2	large eggs
⅓	cup vegetable oil
½	cup packed brown sugar
½	cup grated unpeeled zucchini
½	cup grated peeled carrots
1	teaspoon vanilla extract
1¼	cups whole-wheat flour
¼	cup All-Bran cereal
½	teaspoon salt
½	teaspoon baking soda
1½	teaspoon cinnamon
½	cup chopped walnuts

Preheat oven to 350°F. Grease the bottom of a 9x5-inch loaf pan. In a large bowl, beat eggs, oil and sugar. Stir in zucchini, carrots and vanilla. In a separate bowl, combine flour, All-Bran, salt, baking soda, cinnamon and nuts; add to egg mixture and stir until blended. Pour batter into pan. Bake for about 60 minutes, or until a toothpick inserted in the center comes out clean. Remove bread from oven and cool in pan for 15 minutes. Remove bread from pan and finish cooling on a wire rack.

BASIC QUICK BREAD – CAKE TYPE
Makes 1 Loaf

A quick bread with a moist, very fine, cake-like texture that features flavor variations from applesauce to zucchini.

1¾	cups all-purpose flour
½	teaspoon salt
1	teaspoon baking soda
1	teaspoon cinnamon
¼	teaspoon nutmeg
¼	teaspoon ground cloves
3	large eggs
½	cup vegetable oil
¾	cup sugar
1	teaspoon vanilla extract
¾	cup applesauce

Preheat oven to 350°F. Grease the bottom of a 9x5-inch loaf pan. In a bowl, sift or stir together flour, salt, baking soda, cinnamon, nutmeg and cloves. In a separate bowl, beat eggs, oil and sugar until light and fluffy. Add vanilla and applesauce; mix 30 strokes with a spoon or 30 seconds with a mixer at low speed. Mix flour mixture into egg mixture, using about 30 strokes or 30 seconds at low speed. Pour batter into pan. Bake for 65-70 minutes, or until a toothpick inserted in the center comes out clean. Remove bread from oven and cool in pan for 10 minutes. Remove bread from pan and finish cooling on a wire rack.

VARIATIONS:
- BANANA BREAD: Omit cinnamon, nutmeg and cloves. Increase sugar to ¾ cup + 3 tablespoons. Substitute 1 cup mashed banana for the applesauce.
- PUMPKIN BREAD: Decrease baking soda to ½ teaspoon. Add ½ teaspoon baking powder. Decrease cinnamon to ½ teaspoon. Increase ground cloves to ½ teaspoon. Increase sugar to ¾ cup + 3 tablespoons. Substitute 1 cup cooked or canned pumpkin purée for the applesauce.
- ZUCCHINI BREAD: Decrease baking soda to ½ teaspoon. Add ½ teaspoon baking powder. Increase sugar to ¾ cup + 3 tablespoons. Omit nutmeg and cloves. Substitute 1 cup packed grated unpeeled zucchini for the applesauce.

BASIC QUICK BREAD – MUFFIN TYPE
Makes 1 Loaf

Lower in sugar and fat than many fruit or vegetable quick breads, this version has a moist, coarse-grained texture.

2	large eggs
½	cup sugar
⅓	cup vegetable oil
¼	cup milk
1	teaspoon vanilla extract
2	cups all-purpose flour
1	teaspoon baking powder
½	teaspoon baking soda
¾	teaspoon salt
1	teaspoon cinnamon
½	teaspoon nutmeg
1	cup applesauce

Preheat oven to 350°F. Grease the bottom of a 9x5-inch loaf pan. In a large bowl, mix eggs, sugar, oil, milk and vanilla. In a separate bowl, sift or stir together flour, baking powder, baking soda, salt, cinnamon and nutmeg; stir into egg mixture until blended. Mix in applesauce. Pour batter into pan. Bake for 50-60 minutes, or until a toothpick inserted in the center comes out clean. Remove bread from oven and cool in pan for 10 minutes. Remove bread from pan and finish cooling on a wire rack.

VARIATIONS:
- BANANA BREAD: Substitute 1 cup mashed banana for the applesauce.
- CARROT BREAD: Omit vanilla. Increase milk to ⅓ cup. Substitute 1 cup grated carrot for the applesauce. Add 2 teaspoons grated orange or lemon zest (optional).
- ZUCCHINI BREAD: Omit vanilla. Substitute 1 cup packed grated unpeeled zucchini for the applesauce. Add 2 teaspoons grated orange or lemon zest (optional).

GINGERBREAD
Makes One 9x9-inch Cake

2⅓ cups sifted all-purpose flour
¾ teaspoon baking soda
¼ teaspoon cinnamon
¼ teaspoon nutmeg
¼ teaspoon allspice
1 teaspoon ground ginger
½ cup sugar
⅓ cup vegetable oil
2 large eggs
¾ cup molasses
⅔ cup water

Preheat oven to 350°F. Grease and flour the bottom of a 9x9-inch baking pan. Mix and sift flour, baking soda, cinnamon, nutmeg, allspice, ginger and sugar into a bowl. Add oil, eggs, molasses and water; beat for 30 seconds with a mixer at low speed, scraping the bowl frequently, until well combined. Pour batter into pan. Spread batter from center so it is slightly higher at the edges. Bake for 40-45 minutes, or until a toothpick inserted in the center comes out clean. Remove from oven. Leave in the pan and cut into squares. Serve warm.

ALTITUDE ADJUSTMENTS:
6,500-8,500 feet: Decrease baking soda to ½ teaspoon.
Raise oven temperature to 375°F.
8,500+ feet: Decrease baking soda to ½ teaspoon. Decrease sugar to ⅓ cup.
Raise oven temperature to 375°F.

RASPBERRY ALMOND COFFEE CAKE

Makes One 8-inch Cake

1	cup all-purpose flour
⅓	cup sugar
½	teaspoon baking powder
¼	teaspoon baking soda
⅛	teaspoon salt
½	cup plain low-fat yogurt
2	tablespoons butter, melted
1	teaspoon vanilla extract
1	large egg
1	cup fresh raspberries
1	tablespoon brown sugar
1	tablespoon sliced almonds
¼	cup powdered sugar, sifted
1	teaspoon skim milk
¼	teaspoon almond extract

Preheat oven to 350°F. Grease an 8-inch round cake pan. In a large bowl, sift together flour, sugar, baking powder, baking soda and salt. In a small bowl, combine yogurt, melted butter, vanilla and egg. Add the yogurt mixture to the flour mixture; stir until just moistened.

Spoon ⅔ of the batter into pan; spread evenly. Combine raspberries and brown sugar; sprinkle over batter and spread to within ½-inch of the edge of the pan. Dollop remaining batter by small spoonfuls over raspberry mixture (the batter will not completely cover the raspberries). Top with the almonds. Bake for 30-40 minutes, or until the top is golden and a toothpick inserted in the center comes out clean. Remove pan from oven and let cake cool for 10 minutes on a wire rack.

While the cake is cooling, make a glaze by combining powdered sugar, milk and almond extract; stir until smooth (if needed, add enough additional milk to form a drizzling consistency). Remove cake from pan and drizzle the glaze over the cake. Serve the cake warm or at room temperature.

—Recipe courtesy of the Derby Hill Inn,
Colorado Bed & Breakfast Cookbook

PEAR WALNUT COFFEE CAKE
Makes One 8x8-inch Cake

1	stick (½ cup) butter or margarine
¾	cup white sugar
1	teaspoon vanilla extract
1	large egg
2	cups flour
1	teaspoon baking soda
1	teaspoon baking powder
½	teaspoon salt
1	cup plain yogurt
3	cups peeled, chopped pears (about 4 pears)
1	cup packed brown sugar
1½	teaspoons cinnamon
½	stick butter, softened
1	cup chopped walnuts

Preheat oven to 350°F. Grease an 8x8-inch baking pan. In a large bowl, cream together butter and white sugar. Stir in vanilla and egg. In a small bowl, combine flour, baking soda, baking powder and salt. Stir yogurt and flour mixture alternately, ⅓ at a time, into the butter mixture, mixing after each addition. Fold in the pears. Pour into pan.

Combine brown sugar, cinnamon, butter and walnuts; sprinkle over batter. Bake for 40-50 minutes, or until a toothpick inserted in the center comes out clean.

—Recipe courtesy of First Fruits Organic Farms,
Colorado Farmers' Market Cookbook

QUICK COFFEE CAKE
Makes One 9-inch Cake

A quick and easy coffee cake. Make it plain or try the fruit variation.

2	cups all-purpose flour
½	cup sugar
¾	teaspoon salt
2	teaspoons baking powder
1	teaspoon nutmeg or cinnamon
1	large egg, beaten
1	cup milk
¼	cup vegetable oil
1	teaspoon vanilla extract
	Topping (recipe follows)

Preheat oven to 375°F. Grease the bottom and sides of a 9-inch round cake pan. In a large bowl, mix flour, sugar, salt, baking powder and nutmeg or cinnamon. In a separate bowl, combine egg, milk, oil and vanilla. Add egg mixture to flour mixture; mix about 20 quick strokes by hand. Pour batter into pan. Sprinkle topping over batter. Bake for 20-25 minutes, or until a toothpick inserted in the center comes out clean. Remove cake from oven and cool in pan on a wire rack.

TOPPING	
¼	cup sugar
½	teaspoon cinnamon
1	tablespoon butter or margarine, softened

Combine all ingredients.

VARIATION
- FRUIT COFFEE CAKE: Increase topping ingredients to ½ cup sugar, 2 teaspoons cinnamon and 2 tablespoons butter or margarine. Prepare batter as directed above. Spread ½ of batter in pan. Arrange 1½ cups sliced peeled apples, peaches, apricots or banana in rows on top of batter. Sprinkle with ½ of topping mixture. Pour remaining batter into pan. Sprinkle with remaining topping. Bake for 30-35 minutes, or until a toothpick inserted in the center comes out clean.

WHOLE WHEAT APPLESAUCE COFFEE CAKE
Makes One 9x9-inch Cake

A moist, flavorful morning treat.

⅓	cup butter or margarine, melted
1½	cups applesauce
1	large egg
¾	cup packed brown sugar
1½	cups whole-wheat flour
¾	teaspoon baking soda
1½	teaspoons cinnamon
½	teaspoon allspice
½	teaspoon salt
½	cup raisins
	Topping (recipe follows)

Preheat oven to 375°F. Grease the bottom of a 9x9-inch baking pan. In a medium bowl, combine melted butter, applesauce, egg and brown sugar; mix well. In a large bowl, sift or stir together whole-wheat flour, baking soda, spices and salt. Add butter mixture to flour mixture; mix well. Stir in raisins. Pour batter into pan. Sprinkle topping over batter. Bake for about 45 minutes, or until a toothpick inserted in the center comes out clean and the top springs back when lightly touched in the center.

TOPPING	
¼	cup packed brown sugar
2	tablespoons whole-wheat flour
⅛	teaspoon cinnamon
⅛	teaspoon nutmeg
1	tablespoon butter or margarine, softened
¼	cup chopped walnuts

Combine all topping ingredients.

BASIC MUFFINS WITH TEN VARIATIONS
Makes 12 Muffins

Serve these basic muffins, or one of the 10 variations, to perk up any meal.
Perfect muffins require little stirring – the batter should be lumpy.

2	cups all-purpose flour
¼	cup sugar
2	teaspoons baking powder
¾	teaspoon salt
1	large egg, beaten
1	cup milk
1	teaspoon vanilla extract
¼	cup vegetable oil

Preheat oven to 425°F. Grease muffin cups. In a bowl, combine flour, sugar,
baking powder and salt. Make a well in the center of flour mixture. In a separate bowl, combine egg, milk, vanilla and oil; add to the well in the flour mixture and stir quickly with a fork until flour mixture is moistened, about 10-15
strokes. Fill muffin cups ⅔-full. Bake for 20-25 minutes, or until golden brown.
Serve warm.

VARIATIONS:
- ORANGE MUFFINS: Substitute ½ cup orange juice for ½ cup of the milk.
  Substitute 1 teaspoon baking powder and ½ teaspoon baking soda for the
  baking powder.
- DATE NUT MUFFINS: Add ½ cup chopped walnuts and ½ cup chopped
  dates during final 7 strokes of mixing.
- JAM OR JELLY SURPRISE MUFFINS: Prepare basic recipe. Fill muffin cups
  ⅓-full. Add 1 teaspoon jam or jelly to the center of each muffin cup. Top
  with remaining batter, filling muffin cups ⅔-full.
- APPLE SPICE MUFFINS: Add ¼ teaspoon allspice to the flour mixture. Stir
  1 cup diced peeled apple and ¼ cup raisins into batter during final 7 strokes.
- WHOLE WHEAT HONEY MUFFINS: Substitute whole-wheat flour for part or
  all of the all-purpose flour. Add ¼ teaspoon baking soda to the flour mixture. Substitute ¼ cup honey for the sugar. Increase milk to 1½ cups.

- BRAN MUFFINS: Decrease flour to 1 cup. Soak 2 cups bran flakes in the milk for 1-2 minutes to soften. Mix bran flake mixture into egg and oil, then add to the flour mixture.
- BLUEBERRY MUFFINS: Lightly fold 1½ cups fresh, frozen or well-drained canned blueberries into batter during last 7 strokes of mixing.
- CORNMEAL MUFFINS: Substitute 1 cup corn meal for 1 cup of the flour. Substitute ½ teaspoon baking soda and 1 teaspoon baking powder for the baking powder. Substitute 1 cup buttermilk for the milk.
- CORN FRITTER MUFFINS: Substitute ½ teaspoon baking soda and 1 teaspoon baking powder for the baking powder. Mix 1½ cups well-drained canned corn and 1 tablespoon chopped pimento into egg mixture.
- OATMEAL MUFFINS: Decrease flour to 1 cup. Soak 1 cup old-fashioned rolled oats in the milk for 15 minutes. Blend oatmeal mixture into egg and oil.

STRAWBERRY CHOCOLATE CHIP MUFFINS
Makes 18 Muffins

1	stick (½ cup) butter
1	cup sugar
2	extra large eggs
2	cups all-purpose flour
1½	teaspoons baking powder
½	teaspoon salt
1	cup milk
1½	cups sliced fresh or unsweetened frozen strawberries
½	cup chocolate chips, or more to your taste

Preheat oven to 400°F. Grease muffin cups. Cream butter and sugar together in a large bowl. Mix in eggs, one at a time. In a separate bowl, combine flour, baking powder and salt. Mix flour mixture and milk alternately, ⅓ at a time, into butter mixture. Stir in chocolate chips and strawberries. Pour batter into muffin cups. Bake for 22 minutes, or until finger pressure does not make an indentation.

—Recipe courtesy of Melissa Craven

PUMPKIN MUFFINS WITH STREUSEL TOPPING
Makes 24 Muffins

3½ cups flour
1 cup packed light brown sugar
1 tablespoon baking powder
1½ teaspoons cinnamon
1 teaspoon salt
1 teaspoon nutmeg
1¼ cups cooked or canned pumpkin purée
2 large eggs, beaten
1 cup milk
⅔ cup vegetable oil
8 ounces cream cheese, divided into 24 pieces
   Streusel topping (recipe follows)

Preheat oven to 375°F. Line muffin cups with paper liners. Sift flour, brown sugar, baking powder, cinnamon, salt and nutmeg together into a bowl. In a separate bowl, combine pumpkin and eggs. Mix the milk and oil into the pumpkin mixture. Add the flour mixture to the pumpkin mixture; stir just until moistened. Fill muffin cups ½-full. Put 1 piece of cream cheese on the batter in each muffin cup, then top with the remaining batter. Sprinkle with the streusel topping. Bake for 20-25 minutes, or until lightly browned. Refrigerate leftover muffins.

STREUSEL TOPPING
½ cup packed brown sugar
1 teaspoon cinnamon
2 tablespoons butter, melted
½ cup finely chopped walnuts

Mix streusel ingredients together with a fork.

—Recipe courtesy of Tigges Farm, *Colorado Farmer's Market Cookbook*

MORNING GLORY MUFFINS
Makes 12 to 18 Muffins

1	cup golden raisins
	Hot water to soak raisins
2	cups all-purpose flour
1	cup sugar
2	teaspoons baking soda
2	teaspoons cinnamon
½	teaspoon salt
2	cups grated carrot
1	tart green apple, peeled and diced
½	cup sliced almonds
½	cup shredded coconut
3	large eggs
⅔	cup butter, melted and cooled
2	teaspoons vanilla extract

Preheat oven to 350°F. Cover raisins with hot water and let soak for 20-30 minutes; drain well. Grease muffins cups, or use paper liners. In a large bowl, sift together flour, sugar, baking soda, cinnamon and salt. Add drained raisins, carrots, apple, almonds and coconut; stir to combine. In a small bowl, whisk together eggs, butter and vanilla. Add the egg mixture to the flour mixture; stir just enough to combine (do not overmix). Spoon batter into muffin cups, filling cups about ¾-full. Bake for 20-25 minutes. Remove muffins from oven and let cool in the pan for 5 minutes. Remove muffins from muffin cups. Serve warm or cooled.

—Recipe courtesy of the Derby Hill Inn,
Colorado Bed & Breakfast Cookbook

BLUEBERRY CREAM MUFFINS
Makes 12 Muffins

2	large eggs
1	cup sugar
½	cup vegetable oil
½	teaspoon vanilla extract
2	cups flour
½	teaspoon salt
½	teaspoon baking soda
1	teaspoon baking powder
1	cup sour cream
1	cup fresh blueberries (or strawberries or raspberries)

Preheat oven to 400°F. Grease and flour muffin cups. In a large bowl, beat eggs with a mixer at low speed. While beating, slowly add sugar, then slowly add oil and vanilla. Sift together flour, salt, baking soda and baking powder into a separate bowl. Mix flour mixture and sour cream alternately into egg mixture, ⅓ at a time. Gently fold in blueberries. Spoon batter into muffin cups. Bake for about 20 minutes, or until golden brown.

NOTE: These muffins are great with fresh berries. If using frozen berries, do not let them thaw – instead add 5-8 minutes to the baking time.

—Recipe courtesy of the *Colorado Bed & Breakfast Cookbook*

SCONES, BISCUITS, PANCAKES & MORE

APRICOT STREUSEL SCONE

Makes 12 Scones

1¼ cups all-purpose flour
½ cup quick-cooking oats
3 tablespoons sugar
¼ teaspoon salt
2½ teaspoons baking powder
⅓ cup butter, chilled
2 large eggs, beaten (reserve 1 tablespoon)
¼ cup low-fat sour cream
½ cup dried apricots, chopped
1 tablespoon 2% milk
Streusel topping (recipe follows)

Preheat oven to 350°F. Combine flour, oats, sugar, salt and baking powder. Using a pastry blender or 2 knives, cut butter into flour mixture until mixture looks like fine crumbs. Stir in eggs (reserve 1 tablespoon of beaten egg to glaze the scones), sour cream, apricots and milk. Turn dough onto a lightly floured surface. Knead lightly 10 times.

Roll or pat dough into a 10x11-inch rectangle. Cut into two 5x11-inch pieces. Lightly pat streusel onto one piece of dough; cover with the other piece of dough. With a sharp knife, cut dough into 12 triangles. Put scones on an ungreased baking sheet. Brush with reserved 1 tablespoon of beaten egg. Bake for 10 minutes, or until golden brown. Immediately remove scones from baking sheet and cool on a wire rack.

STREUSEL TOPPING
1 tablespoon butter, softened
3 tablespoons packed brown sugar
1 tablespoon flour
1 tablespoon quick-cooking oats

Mix streusel ingredients with a fork.

—Recipe courtesy of the Wheat Foods Council

RAISIN STREUSEL SCONES

Makes 12 Scones

1¼ cups all-purpose flour
½ cup quick-cooking oats
3 tablespoons packed brown sugar
¼ teaspoon salt
2½ teaspoons baking powder
⅓ cup butter, chilled
2 large eggs, beaten (reserve 1 tablespoon)
¼ cup low-fat sour cream
⅓ cup raisins
1 tablespoon 2% milk
Streusel filling (recipe follows)

Preheat oven to 350°F. Combine flour, oats, sugar, salt and baking powder. Using a pastry blender or two knives, cut butter into flour mixture until mixture looks like fine crumbs. Stir in eggs (reserve 1 tablespoon of beaten egg to glaze the scones), sour cream, raisins and milk. Turn dough onto a lightly floured surface. Knead lightly 10 times.

Roll or pat dough into a 10x11-inch rectangle. Cut into two 5x11-inch pieces. Lightly pat streusel onto one piece of dough; cover with the other piece of dough. With a sharp knife, cut dough into 12 triangles. Put scones on an ungreased baking sheet. Brush with reserved 1 tablespoon of beaten egg. Bake for 10 minutes, or until golden brown. Immediately remove scones from baking sheet and cool on a wire rack.

STREUSEL FILLING
1 tablespoon butter, melted
3 tablespoons packed brown sugar
1 tablespoon flour
1 tablespoon quick-cooking oats
1 teaspoon cinnamon

Mix streusel ingredients together with a fork.

—Recipe courtesy of the Wheat Foods Council

CRANAPPLE SCONES

Makes 8 Scones

Almost any combination of dried fruit, fresh fruit and/or nuts – such as apricot-almond, strawberry or peach-blackberry – can be substituted for the apples and cranberries in this recipe.

2¼	cups flour
¼	cup + 2 tablespoons sugar
2	teaspoons baking powder
⅜	teaspoon baking soda
¼	teaspoon salt
1	stick (½ cup) + 1 tablespoon unsalted butter, chilled
1	(3-ounce package) cream cheese, chilled
1	large egg, lightly beaten
½	cup buttermilk
⅛	pound frozen and sliced cranberries
⅛	pound apples, peeled and chopped

Preheat oven to 425°F. Combine flour, sugar, baking powder, baking soda and salt in a bowl. Add butter and cream cheese; mix with a paddle or cut in by hand until mixture is crumbly. Add buttermilk and ½ of egg (about 1½ tablespoons); mix just to combine. Stir in cranberries and apples.

Roll out the dough about 1 inch thick. Cut into 8 triangles or rounds. Put scones on a parchment paper-lined or greased baking sheet and brush with the remaining beaten egg. Bake for 20-25 minutes, or until lightly browned. Immediately remove scones from baking sheet and cool on a wire rack.

—Recipe courtesy of Bluepoint Bakery, *Colorado Farmers' Market Cookbook*

CORN BREAD

Makes One 8x8-inch Cornbread

1	cup all-purpose flour
1	cup cornmeal
2½	teaspoons baking powder
1	teaspoon salt
2	tablespoons butter, melted or vegetable oil
2	large eggs, slightly beaten
2	tablespoons sugar
1¼	cups milk (or use ½ milk and ½ buttermilk)

Preheat oven to 425°F. Generously grease an 8x8-inch baking pan. In a large bowl, combine flour, cornmeal, baking powder and salt. Make a well in the center of the flour mixture. In a separate bowl, combine butter, beaten eggs, sugar and milk; add to the well in the flour mixture and stir quickly with a fork just until blended. Pour batter into pan and bake for 20-25 minutes, or until golden brown and a toothpick inserted in the center comes out clean. Serve warm.

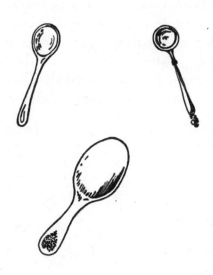

SOUTHWESTERN JALAPEÑO CORN BREAD

Makes 9 Servings

1	cup all-purpose flour
1	cup cornmeal
2½	teaspoons baking powder
2	large eggs, slightly beaten
2	tablespoons vegetable oil
2	tablespoons sugar
1¼	cups milk
⅓	cup chopped dehydrated onion (optional)
1	cup canned cream-style corn
2	tablespoons chopped jalapeño peppers, more or less to taste, or 1 (4-ounce can) chopped mild green chiles
1	cup grated cheddar cheese
⅓	cup crumbled bacon or bacon bits
¼	teaspoon garlic salt
2	tablespoons chopped pimento

Preheat oven to 400°F. Generously grease an 8x12-inch baking or casserole dish. In a large bowl, combine flour, cornmeal and baking powder. Make a well in the center of the flour mixture. In a separate bowl, combine beaten eggs, oil, sugar and milk. Add onion, corn, jalapeño peppers, cheese, bacon, garlic salt and pimentos; mix well. Add egg mixture to the well in the flour mixture; stir quickly with a fork just until blended. Pour batter into baking dish. Bake for 30-35 minutes, or until a toothpick inserted in the center comes out clean. Serve warm.

SOUTHERN BUTTERMILK CORN BREAD

Makes One 8x8-inch Cornbread

½ cup all-purpose flour
1½ cups cornmeal
1 teaspoon salt
1 teaspoon baking powder
½ teaspoon baking soda
2 large eggs, slightly beaten
2 tablespoons vegetable oil
2 tablespoons sugar
1½ cups buttermilk

Preheat oven to 425°F. Generously grease an 8x8-inch baking pan. In a large bowl, combine flour, cornmeal, salt, baking powder, and baking soda. Make a well in the center of flour mixture. In a separate bowl, mix beaten eggs, oil, sugar and buttermilk; add to the well in the flour mixture and stir quickly with a fork just until blended. Pour batter into pan. Bake for 20-25 minutes, or until golden brown and a toothpick inserted in the center comes out clean. Serve warm.

BISCUITS
Makes 15 (2-inch) Biscuits

Handle gently for really delicious biscuits – stir as little as possible and knead lightly.

2	cups all-purpose flour
2	teaspoons baking powder
¾	teaspoon salt
½	stick (¼ cup) butter or margarine, chilled or ¼ cup shortening
¾	cup milk (plus more, if needed)

Preheat oven to 450°F. Sift flour, baking powder and salt into a bowl. Cut butter into flour mixture with a pastry blender or 2 knives until mixture resembles coarse meal. Make a well in the center of the flour mixture. Add the milk to the well; stir with a fork until a soft dough is formed, about 20-30 strokes (add up to 2 tablespoons more milk, if needed to form a soft dough). Form dough into a ball and place on a lightly floured board. Roll dough over and knead lightly 10-15 times. Finish with the unbroken side of the dough on top. Roll or pat out dough to about ½-inch thick and cut with a floured biscuit or cookie cutter. Bake on an ungreased baking sheet for 12-14 minutes.

VARIATIONS:
- CHEESE BISCUITS: Use butter or margarine, not shortening. Mix 1 cup grated cheddar cheese into the flour mixture before adding the milk.
- BUTTERMILK BISCUITS: Substitute ¾ cup buttermilk for the milk. Substitute 1 teaspoon baking powder and ½ teaspoon baking soda for the baking powder.
- WHOLE WHEAT BISCUITS: Substitute ¾ cup whole-wheat flour for 1 cup of the all-purpose flour.
- OIL BISCUITS: Substitute oil for the butter. Combine the oil with the milk and add to the flour mixture.

PANCAKES

Makes Eight (4½inch) Pancakes

1	cup all-purpose flour
1	teaspoon baking powder
½	teaspoon salt
1	tablespoon sugar
1	large egg, beaten
¾	cup milk
2	tablespoons vegetable oil

Preheat a griddle to 375°F or a skillet over medium-high heat. In a bowl, combine flour, baking powder, salt and sugar. In a separate bowl, combine egg, milk and oil. Add egg mixture to flour mixture; stir until smooth. Pour or spoon batter onto hot, slightly greased griddle or skillet. Cook pancakes until golden brown on both sides. Serve immediately or freeze and reheat in a toaster or oven.

VARIATIONS:

- WHOLE WHEAT MOLASSES PANCAKES: Substitute ¾ cup + 2 tablespoons whole-wheat flour for the all-purpose flour. Omit the sugar. Mix 1 tablespoon molasses into the egg mixture.
- WAFFLES: Increase baking powder to 1¼ teaspoons. Add 1 teaspoon vanilla extract. Bake in a preheated waffle iron until golden brown and crisp.

OATMEAL PANCAKES

Makes Ten (4-inch) Pancakes

1	large egg
1¼	cups buttermilk
1	tablespoon honey
2	tablespoons vegetable oil
½	cup old-fashioned rolled oats
⅔	cup whole-wheat flour
2	tablespoons wheat germ
½	teaspoon baking soda
¼	teaspoon salt

Preheat a griddle to 375°F or a skillet over medium-high heat. In a bowl, combine egg, buttermilk, honey and oil; beat well. Add oats, whole-wheat flour, wheat germ, baking soda and salt; stir until well blended. Pour or spoon batter onto hot, slightly greased griddle or skillet. Cook pancakes until golden brown on both sides. Serve immediately or freeze and reheat in a toaster or oven.

VARIATION:
- WAFFLES: Increase oil to ¼ cup. Bake in a preheated waffle iron until golden brown and crisp.

TOASTED ALMOND APRICOT PANCAKES

Serves 4

1	cup all-purpose flour
2	tablespoons sugar
1½	teaspoons baking powder
¼	teaspoon salt
¾	cup sliced almonds, toasted lightly
1	large egg, beaten
1	cup milk
2	tablespoons butter, melted or vegetable oil
	Apricot sauce (recipe follows)

Preheat a griddle to 375°F or a skillet over medium-high heat. In a bowl, combine flour, sugar, baking powder, salt and toasted almonds. In a separate bowl, combine beaten egg, milk and butter or oil. Add egg mixture to flour mixture all at once; stir just until blended. Pour batter, ⅓ cup at a time, onto a hot, lightly greased griddle or skillet. Cook pancakes until golden brown on both sides. Serve with hot apricot sauce.

APRICOT SAUCE

8-0	apricots, peeled and pitted
½	cup sugar (more or less, depending on the sweetness of the fruit)
¼	cup water
1	tablespoon butter

Purée the apricots in a food processor. Pour apricot purée into a saucepan. Add sugar, water and butter. Bring to a low boil over medium heat, stirring frequently. Lower the heat and simmer for 15-20 minutes, until the desired sauce consistency is achieved.

—Recipe courtesy of Melissa Craven

CAKE DOUGHNUTS

Makes 14 Doughnuts

A quick doughnut recipe with an applesauce variation.

	Oil for deep frying
2¼	cups all-purpose flour
2	teaspoons baking powder
¾	teaspoon salt
½	teaspoon nutmeg
¾	teaspoon cinnamon
1	large egg
½	cup sugar
1	tablespoon vegetable oil
½	cup milk
1	teaspoon vanilla extract

Preheat oil to 365-370°F in a heavy saucepan, deep skillet or deep-fat fryer. Sift flour, baking powder, salt, nutmeg and cinnamon together in a medium bowl. Beat egg in a large bowl. Gradually mix in sugar. Mix in oil, milk and vanilla. Add flour mixture; stir until blended. Chill dough for 20 minutes.

Knead dough on a floured board about 4 times. Roll out dough to ⅜-inch thick. Cut into doughnut shapes and fry in hot oil, turning often, until golden brown, about 2½ minutes. Remove doughnuts and drain on paper towels. Roll doughnuts in sugar or cinnamon-sugar, or dip in powdered sugar or a glaze.

VARIATION:
- APPLESAUCE DOUGHNUTS: Substitute ½ cup applesauce for the milk.

CRÊPES

Makes 6 to 8 Crêpes

A thin French pancake to wrap around appetizer, main dish, vegetable or dessert fillings.

1	large egg, beaten slightly
½	cup milk
2	teaspoons butter, melted or vegetable oil
⅓	cup all-purpose flour
¼	teaspoon salt

Combine beaten egg, milk, oil, flour and salt; mix until smooth. If possible, refrigerate the batter for 30-60 minutes or longer before cooking (this allows the flour to absorb more liquid for more tender crêpes).

Heat a greased or nonstick pan over medium to medium-high heat until added drops of water "dance" and sizzle. Pour 2 tablespoons of batter into the center of a 6-inch pan or 3 tablespoons of batter into an 8-inch pan; quickly rotate the pan to the spread batter evenly over the bottom of the pan. Cook on one side only, until bottom of the crêpe is lightly browned, with a lacy look. Loosen edges and carefully lift crêpe from pan to a plate.

VARIATIONS:
- DESSERT CRÊPES: Add 2 teaspoons sugar and ½ teaspoon vanilla extract or other flavoring to crêpe batter.
- WHOLE WHEAT CRÊPES: Substitute 3 tablespoons whole-wheat flour for 3 tablespoons of the all-purpose flour.
- WHEAT GERM CRÊPES: Substitute ¼ cup all-purpose flour and 4 teaspoons wheat germ for the flour.
- CORN MEAL CRÊPES: Substitute 3 tablespoons corn meal and 3 tablespoons all-purpose flour for the flour.

CREAM PUFFS *Makes 18 Medium Cream Puffs*

Elegant, yet simple to make, cream puffs can be used with sweet or savory fillings. Cream puffs freeze well.

1	cup all-purpose flour
⅛	teaspoon salt
1	tablespoon sugar
1	cup water
⅓	cup butter or margarine
4	large eggs

Preheat oven to 425°F. Lightly grease a baking sheet. Mix together flour, salt and sugar. Bring water and butter to a boil in a heavy saucepan. Lower the heat, add flour mixture and cook, stirring constantly with a wooden spoon, until mixture forms a smooth, dry paste that does not cling to the sides of the spoon or the pan (do not overcook). Remove pan from heat and cool for 2 minutes.

Add the eggs to the flour mixture in the saucepan, one at a time, beating thoroughly after each addition. (The dough should no longer look "slippery" and should stand erect when scooped up on a spoon after the last egg has been incorporated.) Spoon or drop dough in desired shapes onto baking sheet. Sprinkle a few drops of water over each cream puff. Bake for 20 minutes. Turn off the oven and let the cream puffs sit in the oven for 20 minutes before removing. When cream puffs are completely cool, slice in half and fill with custard, pudding, ice cream, yogurt or tuna or chicken salad.

FLOUR TORTILLAS *Makes Eight 11-inch or Eleven 7-inch Tortillas*

2	cups all-purpose flour
¾	teaspoon baking powder
1	teaspoon salt
¼	cup shortening
¾	cup warm water

Preheat a griddle or an electric frying pan to 380°F or a skillet over medium-high heat. Stir together flour, baking powder and salt. Cut in shortening with a fork or pastry blender until mixture is crumbly. Add warm water to make a medium-stiff dough. Form dough into a ball; knead on a lightly floured surface until smooth and flecked with air bubbles. Form into balls and roll out into very thin circles. Place tortillas on hot ungreased griddle or skillet; cook until lightly browned with flecks on one side, about 20 seconds. Turn and cook the other side until lightly browned with flecks.

POPOVERS *Makes 11 Medium Popovers*

1	cup sifted all-purpose flour
1	teaspoon sugar
¼	teaspoon salt
1	cup milk
2	large eggs
1	tablespoon butter or margarine, melted

Preheat oven to 450°F. Grease popover or deep muffin cups. Sift together flour, salt and sugar into a bowl. In a separate bowl, combine milk, eggs and butter; add to flour mixture and beat until smooth and well blended. Pour batter into popover or muffin cups, filling each cup ½-full. Bake for 15 minutes. Lower oven temperature to 325°F and bake for 25 more minutes, until popover "side walls" are firm and popovers are well browned.

VARIATION:
- CHEESE POPOVERS: Grate ½ cup cheddar or Parmesan cheese. Put 1 tablespoon of popover batter into each popover cup. Sprinkle with a few teaspoons of grated cheese and top with 1 more tablespoon of batter.

MAKING
YEAST BREADS AT
HIGH ALTITUDE

INTRODUCTION

Baking yeast breads in home kitchens need not be too difficult or time-consuming. A good loaf of bread is well shaped, evenly rounded, has good volume and is reasonably light. The crust is a rich, golden brown, the top somewhat deeper brown than the sides and bottom. The crust is smooth and free from wrinkles and bulges. The texture is reasonably fine, even and free from streaks. The flavor is fresh and nutty.

The yeast dough recipes in this chapter are designed for home bakers who have relatively short periods of time to spend in the kitchen. Once made, the dough can be refrigerated for up to five days. Some basic facts are given here about the ingredients that go into breads and the importance of the various bread making steps. This information, together with recipes adjusted for high altitude, may help make the job of baking yeast breads at high altitudes easier and the results better and more certain.

INGREDIENTS

Plain breads and rolls are made from flour, liquid, yeast, fat, salt and sugar. Eggs, fruit, nuts, spices and other ingredients may be used in rolls, coffee cakes and specialty breads.

Flour: All-purpose flour is most commonly available, but bread flour will yield the finest loaf. Bread flour has a higher protein content than all-purpose flour and is designed to yield a premium yeast product. All-purpose flours are generally prepared from blends of hard wheat. For increased fiber content, variety or for different flavors and textures, whole-wheat, rye and other kinds of flour may be used in place of part or all of the all-purpose or bread flour in a recipe.

In bread recipes, the given flour measurements are the approximate amounts needed to make dough of the proper consistency. The actual amount of flour needed per cup of liquid will depend on the kind of flour used, how much the flour has dried out and whether or not the flour is sifted. Different kinds of flours tend to absorb different amounts of liquid. Flours also dry out in arid climates and at high altitudes.

Liquid: Liquid in yeast doughs and batters may be milk, water, potato water (water in which potatoes have been cooked) or certain fruit juices. Milk gives a good color and flavor to breads and improves the nutritional value.

The type of milk used may be liquid milk, evaporated milk or non-fat dry milk solids. Dilute evaporated milk with an equal amount of water. Non-fat dry milk solids reconstituted with hot water are a convenient replacement for warmed liquid milk in bread recipes. Substitute ⅓ cup dry milk solids and 1 cup of hot water (105-115°F) for each 1 cup of liquid milk.

Yeast: Yeast produces carbon dioxide, the leavening gas that causes batters and doughs to rise. One envelope (2½ teaspoons) of active dry yeast and one small (⅝-ounce) cake of compressed yeast may be used interchangeably. The amount of yeast used will affect the speed of rising. Sea level recipes vary in the amount of yeast recommended, from ½-2 envelopes or small cakes per cup of liquid. The smaller amount is sufficient at high altitudes, particularly if adequate time is allowed for rising. Using the larger amount speeds the bread-making process, perhaps even making it too fast at high altitude. At high altitudes, using less yeast than called for in a recipe developed at sea level helps to equalize the difference in the time required for a yeast dough to double in size. This is important because rising too fast will not allow enough time for full flavor development. Use active dry yeast or compressed-type yeast, but make sure it's fresh (check the expiration date printed on the back of the package of active dry yeast).

Fat: Fat adds flavor and makes the bread tender and the crumb silky. Shortening, oils, butter or margarine are suitable fats to use in breads.

Salt: Salt adds flavor and helps control the action of the yeast.

Sugar: Sugar speeds the activity of the yeast and gives flavor to the bread and color to the crust.

Eggs: Eggs add flavor and nutritional value, but they also improve the color, texture and structure of many yeast products such as rolls and coffee cakes.

PROCEDURE

Mixing: The straight-dough method of mixing is given in the recipes in this chapter. This procedure saves time because all of the ingredients are mixed together at once, and then the dough is allowed to rise. With this method, yeast is softened and activated for 5-10 minutes in ¼ cup of warm water (105-115°F) for active dry yeast (95°F water for compressed yeast) prior to adding it to the batter. (If you do not have a thermometer, let a few drops of water fall on your wrist. The water should feel slightly warm for active dry yeast and slightly cool for compressed yeast.)

The rapid-mix method is a variation of the straight-dough method, in which undissolved yeast is mixed with part of the flour and other dry ingredients. Very hot water and/or milk (120-130°F) is then added. Rapid-mix doughs rise faster because warmer liquids are used. The key to success with this method is making sure that each yeast granule is coated with flour before adding the hot liquid.

With either mixing method, stir or beat the dough using a spoon or a mixer at medium-low speed until the gluten strands are stretchy and the dough forms circles around the bowl. Continue adding flour until the dough is stiff and does not cling to the sides of the bowl. Turn out the dough onto a lightly floured pastry cloth or a board. (Softer doughs are easier to handle on a pastry cloth than on a board. Pastry cloths are available at kitchen specialty stores). Guard against working too much flour into the dough by sprinkling no more than 2 tablespoons of flour at a time on the pastry cloth or board. (Doughs that have too much flour are stiff and dry and do not make good breads. Doughs that are too soft and sticky do not make good breads either.) Use enough flour during mixing to form dough that is rough in appearance and can be lifted in a mass from the bowl (adding flour to dough after it has risen causes streaks in the finished products).

Kneading: The main reason for kneading yeast doughs is to develop the gluten. Gluten is the term given to a protein complex that is cohesive, elastic and extensible. It forms when flour is moistened and mixed. Gluten is made up of several different proteins common to wheat. These proteins are insoluble in water and closely related in chemical behavior and structure.

While one is beating, kneading and adding water to a flour mixture, gluten is forming a network of protein strands throughout the dough. Strands of this gluten network hold together both the solid constituents of a flour mixture and droplets of water within the meshes. Since gluten is elastic and tenacious, it stretches to form cells that hold the leavening gas produced in batters and doughs. Under favorable conditions, yeast acts upon sugars present in batters or doughs to produce carbon dioxide, the leavening gas. As the action of the yeast continues, many small bubbles of carbon dioxide accumulate throughout the batter or dough. Numerous tiny bubbles of carbon dioxide, together with an elastic, stretchy gluten, make the texture of a yeast bread fine and light. During baking, carbon dioxide gas expands to make the bread porous, and the gluten hardens to give the bread structure.

The kneading process increases and enhances the cohesive and elastic properties of the gluten strands. These gluten strands then stretch to form thin filaments around the many tiny cells needed to hold the bubbles of carbon dioxide gas as they are formed by the action of the yeast. These gluten filaments do not break, either during rising or baking, but expand as the leavening gas expands.

As the kneading process continues and the gluten develops, the dough should begin to feel "alive" and springy. Knead the dough quickly and easily. Maintain a rhythmic motion and keep your fingers curved. Lift the edge of the dough, then fold the dough over and push down and away from you with the heel of the hand. Give dough about a ¼-turn with each pushing motion and repeat the entire process. Avoid breaking or tearing the dough – it will injure the gluten. If the dough seems resistant or hard to manage, let it rest for 5-10 minutes, then resume kneading. The average time required to knead bread dough is 10 minutes. The actual time varies with the kind of flour, amount of dough and the way in which the dough is manipulated. (As a general rule, there may be more danger of under-kneading than of over-kneading.) When the dough is kneaded enough and the gluten is well developed, the dough will feel "light" and look smooth and satiny. Also, there will be many tiny blisters under the surface of the dough. If you hold your hand lightly on the surface of the dough for 30 seconds, it should not stick to your hand or the board.

Rising: Place dough in a lightly greased bowl. Turn the dough upside down to lightly grease the top surface. Cover with a damp towel or a piece of plastic wrap. Set the bowl in an unheated oven above a pan of hot water to keep the dough warm (80-85°F) during rising. Allow the dough to rise until it has doubled in size (mark the bowl or pan so you can see when the dough has doubled in size.) To test whether the dough has risen enough, press the tip of the first finger into the dough to the second joint, then quickly remove it. This is the "ripe test." If the dent stays in the dough, it is ready to punch down.

Punching Down: Plunge your fist into the middle of the dough. Fold the edges of the dough to the center. Turn the ball of dough upside down. Punching the dough down is important for several reasons: it collapses the gluten; releases excess carbon dioxide; distributes the nutrients more evenly; and brings the yeast in contact with a fresh supply of food and oxygen.

Second Rising: A second rising is recommended for bread doughs made at high altitudes. Doughs double their size more quickly at high altitudes. The higher the altitude, the lower the air pressure and thus, the shorter the time required for the leavening gases to expand and the dough to double in size. Punching the dough down twice at high altitudes allows fermentation to go on long enough to cause the changes in the gluten that make bread tender, light and of good flavor. Take care to punch the dough down before it has risen so much that the cells collapse and the dough falls (this can happen rather quickly at high altitudes). Once a dough falls, the bread will be coarse and of poor quality.

Shaping: Knead risen dough down gently. Let the dough rest for 5 minutes on a floured pastry cloth or board. There are many methods of shaping to produce a rounded, symmetrical loaf. You may wish to follow the directions given here (or use those with the recipe you are using):

1. Roll the dough with a rolling pin into a 10x6-inch rectangle, forcing out any gas bubbles.
2. Beginning with the 6-inch edge, roll the dough toward you jelly-roll style. Push the roll into the dough as you roll to prevent holes from forming.
3. Seal the edge by pinching the edge and the roll together. Seal the ends by pinching them into the roll.
4. Put the loaf in the center of a greased baking pan or baking sheet with the seam underneath, and let rise until doubled in size.

Baking: The best baking temperature depends somewhat on the richness of the dough. Breads increase suddenly in size during the first few minutes of baking because the heat of the oven causes the gases to expand, and fermentation is faster until the heat of the oven deactivates the enzymes. This process is called "oven spring." Bread is done when the crust is golden brown and the loaf has a hollow sound when tapped on the bottom with a finger. If you prefer a softer crust, brush the crust with melted butter or oil as soon as the loaf is removed from the oven. Remove the loaf from the pan soon after it is baked and allow it to cool on a wire rack.

Storage: When bread is cool, wrap it airtight and store in a clean, dry, well ventilated place. Freshly baked bread will keep well at room temperature for a few days. However, it has a tendency to mold in humid environments and to dry out in arid environments. Storing bread in the refrigerator will help prevent molding, but the bread will become stale more quickly. Breads and doughs also may be frozen as directed below.

FREEZING YEAST BREADS AND DOUGHS

Freezing Yeast Dough: Prepare yeast dough as directed. Immediately after the dough rises for the second time, punch down and seal airtight in a freezer bag. Freeze immediately at 0°F. The dough will keep in the freezer for up to 14 days. When ready to use, defrost dough in the freezer wrapping overnight in the refrigerator (dough defrosted at room temperature may be rising on the outside while the inside is still icy – the resultant bread will then be soggy). After defrosting the dough, unwrap, knead down, shape and put in the pan. Allow to rise in a warm place (80-85°F) until doubled in size and bake as directed.

Freezing Baked Yeast Bread: After baking, cool the bread thoroughly. Seal the bread airtight and freeze at 0°F. Bread will stay fresh for up to 3 months at 0°F. Thaw frozen bread in the freezer wrapper for about 1 hour at room temperature. Bread is best if used soon after defrosting.

Freezing Roll Dough: Prepare roll dough as directed. Without letting the dough rise a second time, shape rolls as desired. Immediately place rolls on a metal pan and put in the freezer with the sides of the pan touching the sides of the freezer. The rolls will freeze within about 2 hours, depending on the freezer temperature. Package rolls immediately after freezing to prevent drying out. Choose a container that the rolls will fill almost completely. Close the container, label and store for up to 3 months at 0°F. When ready to bake, remove the rolls from the package, place on a baking sheet, cover with a towel and let rise in a warm place (80-85°F) until doubled in size. Bake as directed.

Freezing Baked Rolls: After baking, allow rolls to cool. Seal rolls airtight, mark and freeze at 0°F. When ready to use, wrap rolls in foil and heat in a preheated 275-300°F oven for 10-15 minutes.

WHITE BREAD
Makes 2 Loaves

1	package (2½ teaspoons) active dry yeast
¼	cup warm water (105-115°F)
5	tablespoons sugar
2	teaspoons salt
½	stick (¼ cup) butter or shortening, softened, or ¼ cup vegetable oil
1¾	cups milk
6	cups sifted all-purpose flour (about)

Dissolve yeast in the warm water. Put sugar, salt and butter in a bowl. Pour in milk; stir until dissolved. Add 3 cups of flour; beat well. Add dissolved yeast; beat until smooth. Thoroughly mix in enough of the remaining 3 cups of flour to make a moderately stiff dough. Turn dough out onto a lightly floured pastry cloth or board. Knead until smooth and elastic. Put dough in a lightly greased bowl. Cover and let rise in a warm place (80-85°F) until doubled in size.* Punch down. Let rise again until doubled in size.* Knead down gently. Let rest on a pastry cloth or board for 5 minutes. Divide dough in half and shape into loaves. Put loaves in greased 9x5-inch loaf pans. Cover and let rise until doubled in size.* Preheat oven to 375°F. Bake for 45-55 minutes.

*Approximate rising times at altitudes of:

	3,500-6,500 feet	6,500-8,500 feet	8,500+ feet
1st rising	60 minutes	45 minutes	40 minutes
2nd rising	30 minutes	25 minutes	20 minutes
3rd rising	30 minutes	25 minutes	20 minutes

VARIATIONS:
- RAISIN BREAD: Sprinkle 1 tablespoon of flour over 1 cup of raisins; add to dough with second 3 cups of flour. Use the above rising times.
- ORANGE BREAD: Decrease milk to 1½ cups. Add ¼ cup of orange juice and the grated zest of 1 orange to milk mixture. Use the following rising times:

*Approximate rising times for Orange Bread at altitudes of:

	3,500-6,500 feet	6,500-8,500 feet	8,500+ feet
1st rising	65 minutes	45 minutes	40 minutes
2nd rising	45 minutes	30 minutes	25 minutes
3rd rising	35 minutes	25 minutes	25 minutes

WHITE BREAD ENRICHED WITH SOY FLOUR AND WHEAT GERM

Makes 2 Loaves

1	package (2½ teaspoons) active dry yeast
¼	cup warm water (105-115°F)
3	tablespoons sugar
1½	teaspoons salt
3	tablespoons butter or shortening, softened, or vegetable oil
1¼	cups warm milk (105-115°F)
4	cups all-purpose flour, sifted (about)
3	tablespoons soy flour
3	tablespoons wheat germ, plus extra for tops of loaves
	Butter, melted (for brushing on loaves)

Dissolve yeast in the warm water. Put sugar, salt and butter in a bowl. Pour in milk; stir until dissolved. Mix 2 cups of all-purpose flour with the soy flour; add to the milk mixture and beat until smooth. Add dissolved yeast; blend well. Thoroughly mix wheat germ and enough of the remaining 2 cups of all-purpose flour to make a moderately stiff dough. Turn out onto a lightly floured board or pastry cloth. Knead until smooth and elastic. Put dough in a lightly greased bowl. Cover and let rise in warm place (80-85°F) until doubled in size.* Punch down. Let rise again until doubled in size.* Knead down gently. Divide dough in half and shape into 2 balls. Let rest on a pastry cloth or board for 5 minutes. Shape into loaves. Put loaves in greased 9x5-inch loaf pans. Cover and let rise until doubled in size.* Preheat oven to 375°F. Brush tops of loaves with melted butter, then sprinkle with wheat germ. Bake for about 45 minutes.

*Approximate rising times at altitudes of:

	3,500-6,500 feet	6,500-8,500 feet	8,500+ feet
1st rising	60 minutes	40 minutes	35 minutes
2nd rising	30 minutes	30 minutes	20 minutes
3rd rising	35 minutes	30 minutes	25 minutes

WHOLE WHEAT BREAD

Makes 2 Loaves

2	packages (5 teaspoons) active dry yeast
½	cup warm water (105-115°F)
¼	cup sugar or honey
2	teaspoons salt
⅓	cup butter or shortening, softened, or vegetable oil
2	cups warm milk (105-115°F)
7	cups whole-wheat flour (about)

Dissolve yeast in the warm water. Put sugar or honey, salt and butter in a bowl. Pour in milk; stir until dissolved. Add 3½ cups of flour; beat well with a spoon or a mixer at medium-low speed. Add dissolved yeast; beat until smooth. Thoroughly mix in enough of the remaining 3½ cups of flour to make a moderately stiff dough. Turn out onto a lightly floured pastry cloth or board. Let rest for 5 minutes. Knead until smooth and elastic. Put dough in a lightly greased bowl. Cover and let rise in a warm place (80-85°F) until doubled in size.* Punch down. Let rise again until doubled in size.* Knead down gently. Let rest on a pastry cloth or board for 5 minutes. Divide dough in half and shape into loaves. Place loaves in greased 9x5-inch loaf pans. Cover and let rise until doubled in size.* Preheat oven to 375°F. Bake for 45-55 minutes.

*Approximate rising times at altitudes of:

	3,500-6,500 feet	6,500-8,500 feet	8,500+ feet
1st rising	55 minutes	45 minutes	40 minutes
2nd rising	30 minutes	25 minutes	25 minutes
3rd rising	30 minutes	25 minutes	25 minutes

HERB BREAD

Makes 2 Loaves

1	package (2½ teaspoons) active dry yeast
¼	cup warm water (105-115°F)
2	tablespoons sugar
1½	teaspoons salt
2	tablespoons butter or shortening, softened, or vegetable oil
¾	cup warm milk (105-115°F)
3½	cups sifted all-purpose flour
2	teaspoons dried sage
2	teaspoons caraway seed
¼	teaspoon ground nutmeg
1	large egg yolk
1	tablespoon cold water

Dissolve yeast in the warm water. Put sugar, salt and butter in a bowl. Pour in milk; stir until dissolved. Add about 1¾ cup of flour; beat well. Add the dissolved yeast, sage, caraway seeds and nutmeg to batter; beat vigorously until smooth. Thoroughly mix in enough of the remaining 1¾ cups of flour to make a moderately stiff dough. Turn out onto a lightly floured pastry cloth or board; knead until smooth and elastic. Put dough in a greased bowl. Allow to rise in a warm place (80-85°F) until doubled in size.* Punch down. Let rise again until doubled in size.* Knead down gently. Divide dough in half and form into 2 balls. Let rest on a pastry cloth or board for 5 minutes. Form loaves by rolling balls under palms of hands. Roll dough from center to ends to form long loaves. Make diagonal slashes about ⅛-inch deep in the tops of the loaves with a sharp knife. Place on a greased baking sheet. Cover with a slightly damp cloth. Let rise until doubled in size.* Preheat oven to 375°F. Beat together egg yolk and cold water; brush lightly on tops of loaves. Bake for about 30 minutes.

*Approximate rising times at altitudes of:

	3,500-6,500 feet	6,500-8,500 feet	8,500+ feet
1st rising	50 minutes	40 minutes	35 minutes
2nd rising	30 minutes	25 minutes	25 minutes
3rd rising	25 minutes	25 minutes	20 minutes

RYE BREAD

Makes 1 Loaf

1	package (2½ teaspoons) active dry yeast
⅓	cup + 1 cup warm water (105-115°F)
1½	teaspoons salt
3	tablespoons sugar
3	tablespoons butter or shortening, softened, or vegetable oil
4	cups unsifted rye flour (about)
1	teaspoon caraway seeds (optional)

Dissolve yeast in ⅓ cup of warm water. Add the remaining 1 cup of water, salt, sugar and butter to dissolved yeast. Add 2 cups of rye flour; beat until smooth with a spoon or a mixer at medium-low speed. Add caraway seeds; beat for 30 seconds. Thoroughly mix in enough of the remaining 2 cups of flour to make a moderately stiff dough. Turn out onto a lightly floured pastry cloth or board and knead about 250 times. Put dough in a greased bowl. Cover and let rise in a warm place (80-85°F) until almost doubled in size.* Punch down dough and knead 100 times. Grease the bottom of a 9x5-inch loaf pan. Shape dough into a loaf; put in pan. Let rise until almost doubled in size.* Preheat oven to 425°F. Bake for 15 minutes. Lower oven temperature to 350°F and bake for about 30 minutes more.

*Approximate rising times at altitudes of:

	3,500-6,500 feet	6,500-8,500 feet	8,500+ feet
1st rising	60 minutes	45 minutes	40 minutes
2nd rising	25 minutes	25 minutes	20 minutes

FRENCH BREAD

Makes 2 Loaves or 1 Loaf and 12 Rolls

5-5½	cups sifted all-purpose flour (about)
1	tablespoon sugar
2	teaspoons salt
1	package (2½ teaspoons) active dry yeast
2	cups very hot water (120-130°F)
1	large egg white, unbeaten

In a large bowl, thoroughly mix 2 cups flour, sugar, salt and yeast. Add hot water and beat for 2 minutes with a mixer at medium speed, scraping the bowl occasionally. Gradually mix in enough of the remaining 3-3½ cups of flour to make a soft dough. Turn dough out onto a lightly floured pastry cloth or board and knead until smooth and satiny, 5-10 minutes. Shape into a smooth ball. Place in a greased bowl, turning once to grease the top of the dough. Cover and let rise in a warm place (80-85°F) until doubled in size, about 60 minutes. Punch down. Divide dough in half and shape into 2 balls. Cover and let rest for 5 minutes.

Rub a little shortening onto the palms of your hands. Starting in the center, roll each ball of dough in your hands to form 2 long, slender loaves, about 3 inches in diameter.* Put loaves 4 inches apart on a lightly greased baking sheet sprinkled with cornmeal. With a sharp knife, cut diagonal slashes about ¼-inch deep and about 1½ inches apart into the top of each loaf. Cover and let rise until a little more than doubled in size, about 60 minutes. Preheat oven to 425°F. Bake for 25-35 minutes. Remove from oven and brush tops of loaves with egg white. Bake for 2 minutes more. Remove loaves from baking sheet and cool on wire racks.

*Another shaping method: On a lightly greased or floured surface, roll each dough ball into an 8x15-inch rectangle. Beginning with the 15-inch side, roll dough toward you, tapering the ends. Seal edges and ends with thumbs or heals of hands. Bake as directed above.

HINT: For a crustier loaf, bake the bread with a shallow pan of water on a lower oven rack.

ONION HERB BRAID

Makes 2 Loaves

This bread is not only delicious, but it looks pretty too. Each strand of the braid is filled with fragrant garlic, onion and herbs. You can freeze the extra loaf if you are not using it right away.

2	packages (5 teaspoons) active dry yeast
¼	cup warm water (105-115°F)
1	stick (½ cup) butter
¼	cup sugar
1½	teaspoons salt
1	cup milk
3	large eggs, beaten
6	cups flour (about)
1	small onion, minced
	Dried thyme or sage
	Garlic powder
1	large egg yolk beaten with 1 teaspoon water
	Sesame seeds (or poppy seeds)

Dissolve yeast in the warm water. Put butter, sugar and salt in a bowl. Heat milk just to the boiling point; pour it over the ingredients in the bowl. Stir until butter is melted. Add yeast mixture and eggs. Add enough flour to make a moderately stiff dough. Knead for 2 minutes. Put dough in a lightly greased bowl, cover and let rise in a warm place (80-85°F) until doubled in size.

Preheat oven to 375°F. Punch down dough and divide it into 2 equal pieces. Cover the first piece until ready to use. Divide the second piece into 3 equal pieces. Form each piece into a long cylinder. Make an indentation along the length of each cylinder and sprinkle some onion, thyme (or sage) and garlic powder into the indentation along the entire length of the cylinder. Bring edges together to seal in the onion, thyme and garlic powder. Braid the cylinders and place on a baking sheet. Repeat with the first piece of dough. Brush tops of braids with the egg yolk mixture. Sprinkle with sesame seeds. Let rise until doubled in size. Bake for 30-35 minutes, or until the bread is golden brown and sounds hollow when tapped on the bottom.

—Recipe courtesy of Janis Judd

HONEY WHEAT BREAD

Makes 2 Loaves or 2 Dozen Rolls

2	packages (5 teaspoons) active dry yeast
½	cup warm water (105-115°F)
2	cups warm milk (105-115°F)
½	stick (¼ cup) butter or margarine, softened
⅓	cup honey
¼	cup packed brown sugar
2½	teaspoons salt
½	cup wheat germ
2	tablespoons wheat gluten (optional)
2	cups whole-wheat flour
2	cups + 1½ cups bread flour (about)

In a large bowl, dissolve yeast in the warm water. Let stand for 10 minutes. Put butter, honey, brown sugar and salt in a bowl. Pour in milk; stir until dissolved. Stir milk mixture into yeast. Add wheat germ, wheat gluten, whole-wheat flour and 2 cups bread flour. Beat for 3 minutes with a mixer at medium-low speed. Stir in enough of the remaining 1½ cups of bread flour to make a stiff dough.

On a lightly floured pastry cloth or board, knead dough for 10 minutes, or until smooth and elastic (dough will be slightly sticky to the touch). Put dough in a lightly greased bowl, turning once to coat the top. Cover and let rise in warm place (80-85°F) until doubled in size, about 75 minutes. Punch down. Let rise again until doubled in size. Grease two 9x5-inch loaf pans. Knead dough down gently. Divide in half and shape into 2 loaves. Put loaves in pan. Cover and let rise in a warm place (80-85°F) until doubled in size, about 1 hour. Preheat oven to 375°F. Bake for 40-50 minutes, or until loaf sounds hollow when tapped on the bottom (to prevent a dark crust, cover loaves with foil during last 15 minutes of baking). Remove loaves from pans. Brush with butter. Cool thoroughly before storing.

VARIATION:
- ROLLS: After dough has risen and been punched down the second time, shape into rolls. Let rise in a warm place (80-85°F) until doubled in size. Bake for about 15 minutes, or until golden.

—Recipe courtesy of the Wheat Foods Council

BAVARIAN SNITZBROD

Makes 6 to 8 Small Loaves

1	cup dried apricots
1	cup prunes
4	tablespoons yeast
½	cup warm water (105-115°F)
1	stick (½ cup) butter, melted or ½ cup vegetable oil
1¼	cups honey
1	teaspoon salt
8	cups whole-wheat flour
1¼	cups golden raisins
1	cup chopped walnuts
2	teaspoons grated lemon zest
1	teaspoon ground cloves
¼	teaspoon ground ginger
¼	teaspoon nutmeg
3	large eggs, lightly beaten

Cover apricots and prunes with water; soak overnight. The next day, drain the apricots and prunes (reserve the soaking liquid), chop and set aside. Add enough water to the reserved soaking liquid to make 3 cups of liquid.

In a large bowl, dissolve yeast in the warm water. Let stand for 5 minutes. Add the 3 cups reserved soaking mixture, butter, honey and salt; mix well. Add 5 cups of flour, 1 cup at a time, mixing thoroughly after each addition. Cover and let rise until mixture is very bubbly. Add the eggs; mix well. Add raisins, walnuts, lemon zest, cloves, ginger, nutmeg, apricots and prunes; mix well. Add enough of the remaining 3 cups of flour to produce a dough that is just slightly sticky. Knead for 10 minutes, then cover and let rise in a warm place (80-85°F) until doubled in size.

Grease 6-8 small (3½x7½-inch) loaf pans. Preheat oven to 325°F. Punch down dough and divide into 6-8 equal parts. Roll each part into a cylinder and place in a loaf pan. Cover the pans and let the dough rise until doubled in size. Bake for 1 hour, or until loaves sound hollow when tapped on the bottom. (Check the loaves after 45 minutes – you may need to cover the tops with foil if they are getting too brown.)

—Recipe courtesy of Mountain Mama Flour,
Colorado Farmer's Market Cookbook

DILLY BREAD

Makes 2 Large or 3 Small Loaves

This is an unusual bread with a coarse texture and delicious flavor. Above 6,000 feet, decrease the yeast to 2 packages (5 teaspoons).

¼	cup chopped onion
2	tablespoons butter
3	packages (7½ teaspoons) active dry yeast
½	cup warm water (105-115°F)
2	cups small-curd cottage cheese
¼	cup sugar
2	teaspoons dill weed
2	teaspoons salt
½	teaspoon baking soda
2	large eggs
5	cups flour (more or less)
	Butter, melted, for brushing on loaves
	Kosher salt

Grease 2 large or 3 small loaf pans. Melt 2 tablespoons butter in a skillet. Add onions and cook over medium heat until soft. In a large bowl, dissolve yeast in the warm water. Thoroughly mix in all of the remaining ingredients (except the melted butter and kosher salt), using enough of the flour to make a stiff dough. Cover and let rise in a warm place (80-85°F) until doubled in size. Punch down and form into loaves. Put loaves in pans and let rise again in a warm place (80-85°F) until doubled in size. Preheat oven to 350°F. Brush the tops of the loaves with melted butter and sprinkle with kosher salt. Bake for about 50 minutes, or until loaves are well browned and sound hollow when tapped on the bottoms.

—Recipe courtesy of Janis Judd

FOCACCIA

Makes 1 Loaf

This versatile, rustic bread can be eaten as is, served with a little olive oil, or slice it in half to make delicious bread for sandwiches. Use your imagination for toppings – try adding fresh rosemary or pitted and sliced olives.

1	package (2½ teaspoons) active dry yeast
½	cup warm water (105-115°F) + ½ cup water
3	cups flour, divided
½	cup olive oil, divided
2	teaspoons salt
1	clove garlic, finely chopped
	Kosher salt
	Chopped fresh basil or rosemary, pitted, sliced kalamata olives, tomatoes (chopped fresh, sun-dried or oven-dried), pesto, Parmesan cheese and/or roasted garlic, for topping (optional)

Sprinkle yeast in the warm water; let stand for 5 minutes to soften, then stir to dissolve. Put 1½ cups of flour in a bowl. Add the yeast mixture; stir to combine. Cover and let rise in a warm place (80-85°F) until doubled in size. Add the remaining 1½ cups flour, ¼ cup of olive oil, ½ cup of water and salt. Cover and let rise again in a warm place (80-85°F) until doubled in size.

Preheat oven to 400°F. Roll dough out on a lightly floured surface to ¼-inch thick. Put dough on a greased baking sheet. Top with the garlic and the optional toppings, if desired. Sprinkle with kosher salt and drizzle with the remaining ¼ cup olive oil. Bake until golden brown.

—Recipe courtesy of Janis Judd

NO-KNEAD OR BATTER BREADS

No-knead or batter breads were developed to simplify making yeast breads and to save time. Coffee cakes, muffins and sweet rolls are the baked goods usually made by this process. No-knead doughs are softer and contain more fat than kneaded doughs. These baked goods are more open-grained, less delicate in crumb and less "nut-like" in flavor than those made from kneaded doughs. No-knead doughs are mixed in the same way as kneaded doughs. Not quite as much flour is used and the gluten is developed by beating. No-knead dough is always allowed to rise once in the pan and then baked.

QUICK NO-KNEAD BATTER BREAD

Makes 1 Loaf or 2 Coffee Cakes

3-3¼	cups all-purpose flour
1½	tablespoons sugar
1	teaspoon salt
1	package (2½ teaspoons) active dry yeast
⅓	cup non-fat dry milk
1	cup very hot water (120-130°F)
2	tablespoons butter or shortening, softened, or vegetable oil
1	large egg, beaten

In a large bowl, thoroughly mix 1 cup of flour, sugar, salt, yeast and dry milk. Gradually add very hot water and butter; beat well with a spoon or beat for 2 minutes with a mixer at medium speed. Beat in egg. Add ¼ cup flour, or enough to make a thick batter. Beat at high speed for 2 minutes, scraping the bowl occasionally. Stir in enough of the remaining 1¾-2 cups flour to make a soft dough (this dough should be softer than a kneaded dough). Cover and let rise in a warm place (80-85°F) until doubled in size, 30-45 minutes. Grease one 9x5-inch loaf pan or two 8x8-inch baking pans. Stir down dough and pat into pan. Cover and let rise until almost doubled in size, about 30 minutes. Preheat oven to 375°F. Bake for 25-35 minutes, or until loaf sounds hollow when tapped on the bottom. Remove bread from pan and cool on a wire rack.

Whole Wheat Batter Bread: Substitute 1¾-2 cups whole-wheat flour for the 1¾-2 cups all-purpose flour added to make a soft dough.

ENGLISH MUFFIN BREAD

Makes 2 Loaves

This batter bread is best sliced and toasted.

5½-6	cups unsifted all-purpose flour
1	package (2½ teaspoons) active dry yeast
1	tablespoon sugar
2	teaspoons salt
⅔	cup non-fat dry milk
¼	teaspoon baking soda
2½	cups very hot water (120-130°F)
	Cornmeal

In a large bowl, mix 3 cups flour, yeast, sugar, salt, dry milk and baking soda. Gradually add very hot water; beat well. Stir in enough of the remaining 2½-3 cups of flour to make a stiff batter. Spoon into two 8½x4½-inch loaf pans which have been greased and sprinkled with cornmeal. Sprinkle tops of loaves with cornmeal. Cover and let rise in a warm place (80-85°F) until almost doubled in size, about 45 minutes. Preheat oven to 400°F. Bake for about 25 minutes. Remove loaves from pans and cool on a wire rack.

VARIATION:
- WHOLE WHEAT ENGLISH MUFFIN BREAD: Substitute 2½-3 cups whole-wheat flour for the 2½-3 cups of all-purpose flour added after the very hot water.

BASIC YEAST ROLLS WITH SIX VARIATIONS
Makes about 3½ Dozen Rolls or 3 Coffee Cakes

1	package (2½ teaspoons) active dry yeast
¼	cup warm water (105-115°F)
1	cup milk
¼	cup sugar (up to ½ cup for sweeter dough)
1	teaspoon salt
½	stick (¼ cup) butter, softened, or ¼ cup vegetable oil
5	cups sifted all-purpose flour, more or less
2	large eggs
1	teaspoon grated lemon zest (optional)

Dissolve yeast in the warm water. Add milk, sugar, salt and butter or oil. Add 2 cups flour. Beat until smooth with a spoon or a mixer at medium-low speed. Add eggs and lemon zest; beat well. Add enough of the remaining 3 cups of flour to make a soft dough. Turn dough out onto a lightly floured pastry cloth or board. Knead until smooth and satiny. Put dough in a lightly greased bowl. Cover and let rise in a warm place (80-85°F) until doubled in size.* Punch down. Let rest for 10 minutes. Shape into rolls. Let rise until doubled in size.* (To test if rolls have risen sufficiently, press a finger lightly on the under side; if the dough retains the dent, it is ready to bake.) Preheat oven to 375°F. Bake for 15-20 minutes.

*Approximate rising times at altitudes of:

	3,500-6,500 feet	6,500-8,500 feet	8,500+ feet
1st rising	75 minutes	55 minutes	45 minutes
2nd rising	35 minutes	35 minutes	30 minutes

VARIATION:
- CINNAMON ROLLS: After basic yeast roll dough has risen once and been punched down, let dough rest for 10 minutes, then roll or pat out into a ¼-inch thick, 8x14-inch rectangle. Brush with 2 tablespoons melted butter or margarine. Sprinkle with a mixture of ¼ cup sugar and 2 teaspoons cinnamon, then sprinkle with ½ cup raisins. Roll up jelly-roll style, starting at the long edge. Cut into 1-inch lengths and place close together in a greased pan, cut-side-down. Let rise in a warm place (80-85°F) until doubled in size.

Preheat oven to 350°F. Brush tops of rolls with melted butter or margarine and sprinkle with more cinnamon-sugar. Bake for 25-30 minutes. If desired, make a glaze by combining 1 cup powdered sugar and ¼ teaspoon vanilla. Stir in 3 tablespoons milk, or enough to reach a spreading consistency. Spread over warm cinnamon rolls to glaze. Serve rolls warm or cool.

- CRESCENT ROLLS: After basic yeast roll dough has risen once and been punched down, let dough rest for 10 minutes, then roll or pat out into 3 circles, each about 10 inches in diameter and ¼-inch thick. Cut into 12 pie-shaped wedges; brush with melted butter. Beginning at the wide edge, roll dough to the point and press together. Curve slightly into a crescent shape; place point-side-down on a greased baking sheet. Cover and let rise in a warm place (80-85°F) until doubled in size. Preheat oven to 375°F. Bake for 15-20 minutes.

- CLOVERLEAF ROLLS: After basic yeast roll dough has risen once and been punched down, let dough rest for 10 minutes, then make small balls of dough so that 3 balls will ½-fill a muffin cup. Dip each ball in melted butter and put 3 balls butter-side-up in each muffin cup. Cover and let rise in a warm place (80-85°F) until doubled in size. Preheat oven to 375°F. Bake for 15-20 minutes.

- FAN-TANS: After basic yeast roll dough has risen once and been punched down, let dough rest for 10 minutes, then roll or pat out into a rectangle about ¼-inch thick. Brush top lightly with melted butter. Cut dough into 1-inch wide strips. Stack 5-8 strips, one on top of another. Cut into 1½-inch long pieces. Place each stack on end in a greased muffin cup. Cover and let rise in a warm place (80-85°F) until doubled in size. Preheat oven to 375°F. Bake for 15-20 minutes.

- PAN ROLLS: Pan rolls are the easiest kind to shape once you learn to make balls of dough of an even size. After basic yeast roll dough has risen once and been punched down, let dough rest for 10 minutes, then roll dough into 1½-inch diameter balls. Put balls in a greased baking pan, allowing each enough space to double in size. Cover and let rise in a warm place (80-85°F) until doubled in size. Preheat oven to 375°F. Bake for 15-20 minutes.

- PARKER HOUSE ROLLS: After basic yeast roll dough has risen once and been punched down, let dough rest for 10 minutes, then roll or pat out ½-inch thick. Cut into rounds with a 2½-inch biscuit cutter. Make an indentation across each round with a table knife. Lightly brush ½ of each round with melted butter. Fold each round in half, butter-side-in. Press outer edges together firmly and place on a greased baking sheet. Cover and let rise in a warm place (80-85°F) until doubled in size. Preheat oven to 375°F. Bake for 15-20 minutes.

WHIRLIGIG ROLLS WITH HONEY TOPPING

Makes 5 Rolls

⅓   recipe Basic Yeast Roll dough (see page 111)
     Honey topping (recipe follows)

Grease a 9-inch round baking pan. After basic yeast roll dough has risen once
and been punched down, let rest for 10 minutes, then roll out ¾-inch thick. Cut
into five 8-inch long pieces. Lay pieces of dough in the shape of wheel spokes in
the pan (see Diagram 1). Roll up each piece of dough, letting each roll slightly
overlap its neighbor (see Diagram 2). Brush with ⅓-½ cup of honey topping.
Let rise in a warm place (80-85°F) until doubled in size, about 30-35 minutes.
Preheat oven to 350°F. Bake for 25-30 minutes.

HONEY TOPPING
½   stick (¼ cup) butter or margarine, softened
2   tablespoons honey, warmed slightly
1   large egg white
1   cup powdered sugar

Cream together butter and honey. Add egg white; mix well. Thoroughly mix
in sugar.

Diagram 1   Diagram 2

CINNAMON BLOSSOM COFFEE CAKE WITH SUGAR CRUNCH FILLING

Makes 1 Cake

⅓   recipe Basic Yeast Roll dough (see page 111)
    Sugar crunch filling (recipe follows)
    Powdered sugar frosting (recipe follows)

After basic yeast roll dough has risen once and been punched down, let dough rest for 10 minutes, then pat or roll into a ½-inch thick, 8x14-inch rectangle. Sprinkle sugar crunch filling evenly over dough. Roll up jelly-roll style, starting at longer edge. Seal the edges and ends. With a sharp knife slice the dough diagonally into 5 equal slices. Put 1 slice in the center of a greased baking sheet. Arrange the 4 remaining slices in a circle around the first slice with each of the slices touching. Cover and let rise in a warm place (80-85°F) until doubled in size, about 30-35 minutes. Preheat oven to 350°F. Bake for 25-30 minutes, or until a toothpick inserted in the center comes out clean. When cool, frost with powdered sugar frosting, if desired.

SUGAR CRUNCH FILLING
¼   cup sifted all-purpose flour
¼   cup packed brown sugar
¼   teaspoon salt
1   teaspoon cinnamon
2   tablespoons butter, chilled
2   tablespoons chopped walnuts

Combine flour, sugar, salt and cinnamon. Cut in butter. Mix in nuts.

POWDERED SUGAR FROSTING
¾   cup powdered sugar
2   tablespoons hot milk (115-125°F)
¼   teaspoon vanilla extract

Blend all ingredients until smooth.

COCONUT PINEAPPLE COFFEE CAKE

Makes One 8x8-inch Coffee Cake

3	tablespoons butter or margarine
2	tablespoons packed dark brown sugar
½	cup shredded coconut
⅓	cup pineapple tidbits, drained
½	recipe Batter Bread (see page 109) or ⅓ recipe Basic Yeast Roll dough (see page 111)

Preheat oven to 375°F. Melt butter in the oven in an 8x8-inch baking pan. Spread brown sugar and coconut evenly over the bottom of the pan. Arrange pineapple tidbits over brown sugar and coconut. Spread batter or roll dough evenly over pineapple. Cover and let rise in a warm place (80-85°F) until doubled in size. Bake for 25-35 minutes, or until a toothpick inserted in the center comes out clean.

ORANGE COFFEE CAKE

Makes One 8x8-inch Coffee Cake

3	tablespoons butter or margarine
¼	cup packed dark brown sugar
1	(11-ounce) can mandarin orange sections, drained
½	recipe Batter Bread (see page 109) or ⅓ recipe Basic Yeast Roll dough (see page 111)

Preheat oven to 375°F. Melt butter in the oven in an 8x8-inch baking pan. Spread brown sugar evenly over the bottom of the pan. Arrange mandarin orange sections on top of brown sugar. Spread batter or roll dough evenly over orange sections. Cover and let rise in a warm place (80-85°F) until doubled in size. Bake for 25-35 minutes, or until a toothpick inserted in the center comes out clean.

CRUMBLE SQUARES
Makes One 8x8-inch Coffee Cake

¼	cup all-purpose flour
¼	cup dry bread crumbs
2	tablespoons sugar
½	teaspoon cinnamon
2	tablespoons butter or margarine, chilled
½	recipe Batter Bread (see page 109) or ⅓ recipe Basic Yeast Roll dough (see page 111)

Grease an 8x8-inch baking pan. Combine flour, bread crumbs, sugar and cinnamon. Cut or rub butter into flour mixture until crumbly. Spread batter or roll dough into the bottom of the pan. Spread topping evenly over batter or dough. Make squares by pressing lines deep into the batter or dough with floured finger tips. Cover and let rise in a warm place (80-85°F) until doubled in size. Preheat oven to 375°F. Bake for 25-35 minutes, or until a toothpick inserted in the center comes out clean.

HONEY TOPPING COFFEE CAKE
Makes One 8x8-inch Coffee Cake

½	stick (¼ cup) butter or margarine, softened
2	tablespoons honey, warmed slightly
1	large egg white
1	cup powdered sugar
½	recipe Batter Bread (see page 109) or ⅓ recipe Basic Yeast Roll dough (see page 111)

Grease an 8x8-inch baking pan. Cream together butter and honey. Add egg white; mix well. Add sugar; mix well. Spread batter or roll dough into the bottom of the pan. Brush top of batter or dough with ⅓-½ cup of the honey mixture. Cover and let rise in a warm place (80-85°F) until doubled in size. Preheat oven to 375°F. Bake for 25-35 minutes, or until a toothpick inserted in the center comes out clean.

REFRIGERATOR YEAST ROLLS

Makes 3-4 Dozen Rolls or Doughnuts, 2 Coffee Cakes or 4 Dozen Sopapillas

This dough will keep for up to 5 days covered and refrigerated. Punch down as needed to prevent the dough from over-rising. Remove the dough from the refrigerator when ready to use. Punch down. Let dough come to room temperature, then shape as desired.

1	package (2½ teaspoons) active dry yeast
1	tablespoon sugar
1	cup warm water (105-115°F)
1	cup milk
7	cups all-purpose flour (about)
2	large eggs, beaten
⅓	cup butter or shortening, softened
½	cup sugar
1	teaspoon salt

In a large bowl, dissolve yeast and sugar in the warm water. Heat milk to just below the boiling point, then cool to lukewarm (80-85°F). Add lukewarm milk and 3 cups flour to the yeast mixture. Beat 130 strokes, or until smooth. Let stand for 30 minutes in a warm place (80-85°F).

Add beaten eggs, butter, sugar, salt and enough of the remaining 4 cups of flour to the yeast mixture to form a soft dough. Knead for 7-8 minutes (about 350 times), until smooth and satiny. Cover and let rise in a warm place (80-85°F) until doubled in size, about 45 minutes. Punch down. Let rest for 10 minutes. Shape into rolls, doughnuts, coffee cakes, etc., as suggested below. Preheat oven to 375°F. Let rise in a warm place (80-85°F) until doubled in size. Bake for about 15 minutes, or until golden brown.

VARIATIONS:
- WHOLE WHEAT REFRIGERATOR YEAST ROLLS: Substitute 3 cups whole-wheat flour for the 3 cups of all-purpose flour added to the yeast mixture with the milk.
- CINNAMON ROLLS: After dough has risen once and been punched down, let rest for 10 minutes, then roll or pat ⅓ of dough into a ¼-inch thick, 6x12-inch rectangle. Brush with 1 tablespoon melted butter. Combine

2 tablespoons of sugar and ½ teaspoon cinnamon. Sprinkle some of the cinnamon-sugar over the dough (reserve some for sprinkling over rolls). Roll up dough jelly-roll style, starting at the long edge. Cut into 1-inch slices. Put slices close together in a greased baking pan, cut-side-down. Let rise in a warm place (80-85°F) until doubled in size. Brush tops of rolls with melted butter or margarine and sprinkle with more of the cinnamon mixture. Preheat oven to 375°F. Bake for about 20 minutes, or until golden brown. Glaze, if desired (see glaze recipe with cinnamon rolls, page 111-112)

- CRESCENT ROLLS: After dough has risen once and been punched down, let rest for 10 minutes, then roll or pat ⅓ of dough into a circle, about 10 inches in diameter and ¼-inch thick. Cut into 12 pie-shaped pieces; brush with melted butter. Beginning at the wide edge, roll dough to the point and press together. Curve slightly into a crescent shape and put rolls, point-side-down, on a greased baking sheet. Brush rolls with melted butter, oil or milk, if desired. Cover and let rise in a warm place (80-85°F) until doubled in size. Preheat oven to 375°F. Bake for about 15 minutes, or until golden brown.

- DOUGHNUTS: After dough has risen once and been punched down, let rest for 10 minutes, then roll out ½-inch thick. Cut into doughnut shapes. Cover and let rise in a warm place (80-85°F) until doubled in size, about 25-30 minutes. Fry in hot deep fat (360°F) until golden brown, about 1-2 minutes per side.

- ROUND DINNER ROLLS: After dough has risen once and been punched down, let rest for 10 minutes, then form ⅓ of roll dough into 14 small balls that are ⅓ of the desired baked size. Grease a 9-inch round baking pan. Put balls close together in pan. Let rise in a warm place (80-85°F) until doubled in size, about 60 minutes. Bake for about 15 minutes, or until golden brown. Remove from oven and rub butter, oil, margarine or garlic-butter over tops of rolls. Sprinkle with Parmesan cheese, if desired.

- SOPAPILLAS: After dough has risen once and been punched down, let rest for 10 minutes, then roll out ⅛-inch thick. Cut into 4-inch squares. Preheat hot deep fat to 360°F (the fat is hot enough when a small piece of dough dropped into it sinks to the bottom of the fryer and then immediately floats to the top). Drop dough squares into fryer and fry until golden brown and puffy, about 1-1½ minutes per side.

BREAD MACHINES

Bread machines are a popular shortcut to fresh goodness. A wide variety of bread machines are available. Each system works a little differently. Whereas all systems have been designed for use at sea level, some offer more flexibility when used at high altitudes. One universal characteristic, however, is that they all operate by a specific mechanism that requires accuracy. This section contains general tips for successful bread machine baking, adjustments for altitude and humidity, and select recipes that have been tested at 5,000 feet, in a low-humidity climate.

Recipes: Most bread machines come with a cookbook of tested recipes. Generally, these recipes are for standard loaves of white, whole-wheat, raisin, French and sweet bread dough. Be creative with these standard recipes by incorporating some of your favorite fruits, vegetables, nuts, seeds or other unique flavors into the dough. Be careful, however, to maintain the balance of ingredients when incorporating additional liquids or grains. Also, to ensure optimal gluten development and even distribution of the ingredients, follow the manufacturer's directions for specific timing requirements when incorporating additional ingredients.

TIPS FOR SUCCESSFUL BREAD MACHINE BAKING

1. Know your machine: Read your bread machine manual and cookbook thoroughly. The tips and hints provide a good trouble-shooting guide. Understand your machine's cycles and select and use them properly.
2. Know your recipe: Read and understand the recipe before you begin.
3. Ingredients: Use fresh, high-quality ingredients and store them properly. Keep whole-grain products, nuts, oils and other perishable ingredients in the refrigerator. Most recipes work best with warm water (105-115°F).
4. Use each ingredient in proper proportion – the relative quantities of ingredients determine the characteristics of the bread.
5. Measure accurately: Manufacturers who include measuring tools with their machines expect you to use them with their recipes. These tools may hold different amounts than standard measuring tools. Check your bread machine's manual or cookbook for the suggested measuring tools.

6. Assemble ingredients in order of use: Many bread machine disasters occur because ingredients were left out or added twice. Assemble ingredients in order of use before adding them. Carefully measure ingredients into the pan, then recheck the list to be sure each ingredient was used.
7. Experiment carefully: For the best results, use tested recipes from a reliable source. When adapting a recipe, change one ingredient type or amount at a time. Never open your machine during rising or baking.

ADJUSTMENTS FOR ALTITUDE AND HUMIDITY

Bread machines are designed for appropriate rising at sea level. As altitude increases, the rising cycle becomes too long and the dough will over-rise. The resulting baked good may have one or more of the following problem characteristics: inflated top (mushroom-like appearance), concave top and sides, decreased volume or coarse texture.

The arid climate at high altitudes also poses a problem. When flour is stored in an arid climate, its moisture content decreases. As a result, you may need to add additional liquid to achieve optimal dough elasticity and protect the motor from stalling. One or more of the following recommendations may be beneficial in troubleshooting altitude and humidity differences:

1. *Yeast:* One way to avoid over-rising and a mushroom-like loaf is to decrease the amount of yeast called for in recipes developed for sea level. One package of active dry yeast contains 2½ teaspoons of dry yeast. In recipes calling for 1 package of active dry yeast, decrease this amount to 2 teaspoons of yeast from 3,500-6,500 feet; 1¾ teaspoons from 6,500-8,500 feet; and 1½ teaspoons above 8,500 feet. At high altitudes, active dry yeast is recommended over "rapid-rise" (fast-acting) yeast. If using rapid-rise yeast, decrease the amount of rapid-rise yeast by ¼-½ teaspoon of yeast per package of active dry yeast called for in recipes developed for sea level.
2. *Salt:* Salt inhibits yeast action and promotes slow rising. An increase from the usual 1 teaspoon of salt to 1½ teaspoons per recipe is recommended for optimal rising without effecting taste.
3. *Liquid:* If the liquid proportion is not adequate to allow the blade to mix, the mixer blade can catch and stall the motor. In arid climates, such as the Rocky Mountain region, additional liquid may be needed to adequately hydrate the flour and make a dough. The actual amount of additional liquid needed will vary with the level of humidity–1-2 additional tablespoons of

liquid per cup of flour is usually sufficient for recipes developed at sea level. Start with the lower amount and add more if needed.

Too much liquid also can present problems. If the bread dough does not clean away from the sides during the final stages of mixing, there is too much liquid in the system. A fallen loaf may be the result of too much liquid or a high level of coarse flours, such as whole wheat or rye. Water, milk, applesauce, fruits, yogurt or vegetables all add liquid to the system. Possible solutions to the "sunken loaf" problem include: reducing liquids by 1 tablespoon at a time, draining canned fruits or vegetables, or substituting bread flour for a portion of the coarse flours.

4. *Gluten:* Below 6,000 feet, a good quality bread flour may be sufficient to supply enough gluten. Gluten should be added above 6,000 feet and when using low-gluten flours such as rye, rice, soy, buckwheat, triticale or amaranth. Use up to 1½ tablespoons of gluten per recipe. Gluten may be difficult to find, but natural food stores often carry it and groceries may special order it.

5. *Lecithin:* Functioning as an emulsifying agent, lecithin helps to stabilize the ingredients and assists in structure formation. It may be used in high altitude bread recipes in addition to gluten. Lecithin is available in liquid or powder form. (Liquid lecithin is thicker than molasses so it may be helpful to use the same measuring utensil in which the oil was measured, to make it slide more easily off the spoon.) The recommended quantity to be used, which has been tested at 6,000 feet, is 1½ teaspoons liquid lecithin for every 1½ tablespoons of gluten used.

6. *Cycle:* Many bread machines have three cycles: white, sweet and French bread. Times for each bread-making step may vary between cycles. Mixing cycles are generally longer for sweet bread relative to white bread. The longer mixing cycle may help to control over-rising by allowing more gluten to develop. In some cases, switching from the "white bread" to the "sweet bread" cycle may be all that is needed to produce high quality bread at high altitude when using a recipe developed for sea level.

BREAD MACHINE PARMESAN CRACKED WHEAT BREAD

Makes 1 Loaf

1½	teaspoons active dry yeast
2	cups whole-wheat flour
1	cup bread flour
¼	cup multi-grain hot cereal
2	tablespoons cracked wheat
2	tablespoons wheat germ
1	teaspoon salt
1	teaspoon dill weed
1	teaspoon dried basil
¼	cup grated carrot
¼	cup grated zucchini
¼	cup grated Parmesan cheese
1	tablespoon vegetable oil
1	tablespoon honey
1	cup warm water (105-115°F)

Add ingredients to bread machine in order listed above. Select the "sweet bread" cycle at a light to medium setting. Set timer, if desired. Press "start" and relax for about 4 hours as your bread kneads, rises and bakes. Upon completion of the baking cycle, most bread machines will "beep." At this point remove the loaf from the bread machine or allow it to remain in the unit for the cooling cycle (if available on your machine). Most bread machines contain a kneading paddle which remains on the bottom of the loaf when it is removed from the pan. This paddle or kneading hook gets very hot so allow the bread to cool prior to removing it. And be certain to remove the paddle before slicing and tasting!

BREAD MACHINE ALMOND BREAKFAST BREAD

Makes 1 Loaf

1½	cups non-fat milk
4	cups bread flour
1	tablespoon gluten
¼	cup almond paste (not marzipan), cut into small pieces
2	tablespoons sugar
1¾	teaspoons salt
2	tablespoons butter or margarine
1	tablespoon almond extract
2	teaspoons active dry yeast
	Glaze (recipe follows)
	Sliced almonds (optional)

Add ingredients to bread machine in order listed above. Select the "sweet bread" cycle. Set timer, if desired. Press "start" and relax for about 4 hours as your bread kneads, rises and bakes. Upon completion of the baking cycle, most bread machines will "beep." At this point remove the loaf from the bread machine or allow it to remain in the unit for the cooling cycle (if available on your machine). Most bread machines contain a kneading paddle which remains on the bottom of the loaf when it is removed from the pan. This paddle or kneading hook gets very hot so allow the bread to cool prior to removing it. Let bread cool and then glaze, if desired. If glazing, top with sliced almonds, if desired.

GLAZE	
1	cup powdered sugar
½	teaspoon almond extract
2-3	tablespoons milk

In a medium bowl, mix powdered sugar, almond extract and enough milk to form a drizzling consistency.

—Recipe courtesy of the Wheat Foods Council

TODAY'S SOURDOUGH AT HIGH ALTITUDE

INTRODUCTION

The history of sourdough dates back to the Egyptians, approximately 6,000 years ago. They discovered that fermented wheat flour would make dough rise, and if they saved some of the fermented mixture, a new batch could be "started." This was the only form of leavening for centuries. In the United States, sourdough is associated with the frontier, where it was a treasured possession that sustained and satisfied westward-bound pioneers, prospectors and settlers for generations.

The sourdough recipes in this chapter have been revised to reflect changes in the lifestyles of many of today's cooks. Short cuts, yeast boosters and convenient methods that might make some traditionalists cringe have been used. Several recipes have been modified to reduce fat, salt and sugar. There are also recipes designed for use with a food processor, dough hook and bread machine.

All of the sourdough recipes in this chapter have been adjusted to use a single basic batter. After you have used 3 cups of the basic batter for bread, there will probably be enough leftover for a cake, cookies or some other baked good that uses a smaller amount. Leftover basic batter may be stored in the refrigerator for 4-5 weeks.

Sourdough starter works best at room temperature. If you use it daily, it can be left loosely covered on a counter. If you don't bake often, you may want to take the starter pot out of the refrigerator once a month and refresh it by adding flour, sugar and water. Let it sit at room temperature for 12 hours, then tightly cover it and refrigerate. A clear tan or gray-to-yellow colored liquid will come to the top when sourdough batter or starter is stored or allowed to stand. When ready to use the batter or starter, simply stir down the liquid into the batter or starter. Discard any starter that turns color (orange or green) or develops unpleasant odors, then make a new starter.

Do not be disappointed if your first attempt at making the starter does not work – try again! Of course, the best way to get a starter is from a friend who has a good one. Some starters are said to be 50-100 years old. If you are fortunate enough to have been given a treasured starter, treat it well – it is a real gift.

MAKING THE BASIC BATTER

STEP 1. *Make one of the following starter recipes:*

YOGURT STARTER

½   cup low-fat or non-fat yogurt (use only a yogurt with live cultures – it
     will state on the side of yogurt container if it contains live cultures)
1   cup flour
1   cup water
1   tablespoon sugar

YEAST STARTER

1   cup lukewarm water (80-85°F)
1   tablespoon sugar
1   cup flour
1   teaspoon yeast or 1 small cake yeast

POTATO WATER STARTER (USE A 1 GALLON CONTAINER)

5   cups flour
2   tablespoons sugar
2   teaspoons salt
4   cups lukewarm (80-85°F) potato water (see recipe on page 128)

Mix ingredients for the above chosen starter in a glass, crockery or plastic container with a lid that can be tightened. If the lid is metal, put plastic film over the top of the container before putting on the lid (no metal should touch the starter). Use a wood or plastic spoon to mix the starter. Let the starter mixture sit at room temperature, with the lid ajar, for 48 hours, or until it has a pleasant, sour odor. Cover tightly and refrigerate, or proceed with Step 2 (page 128).

Commercial starter: Follow package directions, then proceed with the permanent starter pot (page 128) and/or basic batter (page 129)

NOTE: The yogurt and yeast starter recipes make only enough starter for the permanent starter pot. The potato water starter recipe makes enough for the permanent starter pot and the first basic batter.

POTATO WATER (USED FOR POTATO WATER STARTER)	
6	medium to large potatoes, peeled and cut into eighths
5	cups water

Put potatoes and water in a large saucepot. Cover and bring to a boil. Lower heat and simmer until potatoes are easily pierced with a fork. Drain potatoes with a colander into a large bowl. Measure the potato water and add enough tap water to the potato water to make 4 cups of liquid. Let cool to lukewarm (80-85°F) before using in the potato water starter recipe.

STEP 2. *Make a permanent starter pot:*
Making a permanent starter pot is an optional but recommended step. You can make or remake the basic batter used in all sourdough recipes from 1 cup of a pre-made basic batter, 1 cup of a starter or 1 cup of "permanent starter." Since a good starter takes time, effort and sometimes luck to make, and the last cup of a basic batter can be easily used up without thinking, a permanent starter is recommended as an insurance policy. Be sure to make or replenish the permanent starter pot at least 12 hours before making a basic batter recipe. It is advisable to make the starter pot with all-purpose flour. You may make the basic batter with whole-wheat flour.

1	cup Yogurt, Yeast or Potato Starter (see page 127)
1	cup all-purpose flour
1	cup lukewarm water (80-85°F)
1	teaspoon sugar

Mix all ingredients thoroughly in a 2-quart glass, crockery or plastic container. Allow to sit loosely covered at room temperature for 12 hours before using to make the basic batter.

When removing 1 cup of starter to make the basic batter, replenish the starter by stirring 1 cup warm water (105-115°F), 1 teaspoon sugar and 1 cup all-purpose flour into the starter. Allow the starter to sit loosely covered at room temperature for 12 hours before covering tightly and refrigerating.

TIP: Write ingredients and directions for replenishing the permanent starter pot on top of container.

STEP 3. *Make the basic batter:*

1	cup Starter
2½	cups all-purpose flour
1	tablespoon sugar
2	cups lukewarm water (80-85°F)

Combine all ingredients in a large glass or plastic container (gallon glass jars or large plastic containers are good to use – be sure the container is large enough that the batter does not overflow as it produces carbon dioxide and expands). Allow to sit at room temperature, loosely covered, for at least 6 hours or overnight (if using the batter after 6 hours, it's preferable to let it sit for the 6 hours in a warm place (80-85°F) rather than at room temperature). If you are not using the batter right away, or have some left over, cover tightly and refrigerate. Makes about 4 cups.

SOURDOUGH WHITE BREAD

Makes 2 Loaves

2	tablespoons butter or margarine
¾	cup milk
2	tablespoons sugar or honey
1	tablespoon active dry yeast
1	teaspoon salt
4-5	cups all-purpose flour (unsifted)
3	cups Basic Batter

Melt butter in a small pan. Add milk and sugar or honey; stir until dissolved. In a large bowl, thoroughly mix yeast, salt and 4 cups of flour. Add milk mixture and basic batter to flour mixture; stir with a large spoon until well combined. Gradually add up to 1 more cup of flour, kneading in as much as possible. Continue kneading until dough is smooth and elastic, about 8-10 minutes. (An easy test for elasticity is to hold your hand lightly on the surface of the dough for 30 seconds. If it doesn't stick to your hand or the board, it's ready. If it does stick, than it needs more kneading.)

Put dough in a large, lightly greased, warm bowl. Cover and let rise in a warm place (80-85°F) until doubled in size, 45-60 minutes. Punch down and let rise again until doubled in size, 30-45 minutes. Knead down gently. Let rest for 5 minutes, then divide in half and shape into loaves. Grease two 9x5-inch loaf pans. Put dough in pans and let rise until doubled in size, 25-30 minutes. Preheat oven to 375°F. Bake for 45-55 minutes, until the crust is golden brown and the loaf sounds hollow when tapped on the bottom. Cool loaves on a wire rack. For a softer crust, brush the crust lightly with melted butter or oil after removing the loaves from the oven.

NOTE: If you have a mixer, you can expedite the mixing process. Follow the above recipe, but start with 2 cups of flour. Beat dough with a mixer or dough hook for 2 minutes. Using a dough hook or a large spoon, stir in enough of the remaining 3 cups of flour to make a stiff kneaded dough.

VARIATIONS: Whole-wheat or rye flour may be substituted for up to 3 cups of the all-purpose flour. For a sweeter bread, increase sugar or honey to ⅓ cup. For a tasty, hearty bread, use ⅓ cup honey and substitute 1½ cups of a darker flour (whole wheat or rye) for the all-purpose flour.

ONE-RISE BREAD: Below 5,000 feet, you can skip the second bowl rising. Simply punch the dough down after the first rising, shape into loaves and place in greased loaf pans. Let rise until doubled in size, 25-30 minutes, then bake as directed.

SOURDOUGH REFRIGERATOR ROLLS

Makes 36 Rolls

¾   cup water
⅓   cup butter, margarine or vegetable oil
4½-5 cups flour (all-purpose, wheat or a mixture)
1   package (2½ teaspoons) active dry yeast
⅓   cup non-fat dry milk
1   teaspoon salt
⅓   cup sugar
2½   cups Basic Batter

Put water and butter in a small container. Heat until hot (125°F) on stove or in microwave. In a large bowl, combine 1 cup flour, yeast, dry milk, salt and sugar. Stir basic batter and butter mixture into flour mixture by hand. Beat for 2 minutes with a mixer at medium speed. Gradually stir in enough of the remaining 3½-4 cups of flour to make a moderately stiff dough. Turn dough out onto a lightly floured pastry cloth or board. Knead until smooth and elastic. Cover and let rise in a greased bowl until doubled in size. Punch down and cover with oiled or floured plastic wrap. Put a plate on top of the bowl so the dough will not over-rise (the plate may be weighted down with a full soda can or a similar item). Refrigerate for at least 2 hours, or until ready to use (up to 2-3 days). If dough doubles in size in the refrigerator and is not going to be used immediately, punch it down so the gluten strands do not break.

When ready to use, let dough rest at room temperature for 15-20 minutes before kneading down gently and shaping into rolls as desired – fan-tan, cloverleaf, crescent, Parker House, etc. (see page 112 for shaping directions). Let rolls rise until doubled in size. Preheat oven to 375°F. Bake for 20-25 minutes, or until lightly browned. Brushing rolls lightly with butter or oil during the last 5 minutes of baking will aid browning.

FOOD PROCESSOR BREADS

Check to be certain your food processor has a motor with sufficient power to knead dough. Consult the instruction book and/or recipe book for instructions or precautions.

FOOD PROCESSOR SOURDOUGH HONEY WHEAT BREAD

Makes 1 Loaf or 18 Rolls

2½	cups whole-wheat flour (or use all-purpose flour for white bread)
½	teaspoon salt
1	package quick rising yeast or 1 tablespoon active dry yeast
¼	cup honey
3	tablespoons butter, margarine or vegetable oil
⅓	cup water
1	cup Basic Batter

Using the metal blade, process flour, salt and yeast for 5-10 seconds. In a saucepan or medium container, combine honey, butter and water; heat until hot (115°F) on stove or in microwave. Stir basic batter into the honey mixture. Turn on food processor and pour basic batter mixture through the feed tube in a steady stream until a ball forms, about 15 seconds. (If the dough is not stiff enough to form a ball, stop the processor, open and scatter 2-3 tablespoons of flour over the dough. Replace the cover, turn the processor on and a ball should form.) Process for 1 minute more to knead dough (stop the food processor immediately if the dough catches and/or the blade labors or stops).

Carefully remove dough from food processor. Place on a floured surface. Remove blade from processor and place processor bowl over dough, or cover with another bowl. Let dough rest for 10 minutes. Grease a 9x5-inch loaf pan. Shape dough into a loaf and place in pan, or shape into rolls. Cover with oiled wax paper and let rise in a warm place (80-85°F) until doubled in size.

Preheat oven to 375°F. Bake for 35-40 minutes, until crust is golden brown and loaf has a hollow sound when tapped on the bottom. Remove bread from pan and cool on a wire rack. For a softer crust, brush crust lightly with melted butter or oil when the bread comes out of the oven.

FOOD PROCESSOR SOURDOUGH HERB BREAD

Makes 1 Loaf

2⅓	cups all-purpose flour
1	package quick rising yeast or 1 tablespoon active dry yeast
½	teaspoon salt
1½	teaspoons sugar
1	tablespoon crushed dried parsley
½	teaspoon dried minced garlic
1	tablespoon dried minced chives
¼	teaspoon dried basil
¼	teaspoon dried thyme
3	tablespoons butter, margarine or vegetable oil
½	cup water
1	cup Basic Batter

With the metal blade, process flour, yeast, salt, sugar, parsley, garlic, chives, basil and thyme for 5-10 seconds. In a saucepan or medium container, combine butter and water; heat until hot (115°F) on stove or in microwave. Stir basic batter into the butter mixture. Turn on food processor and pour basic batter mixture through feed tube in a steady stream until a ball forms, about 15 seconds. (If dough is not stiff enough to form a ball, stop processor, open and scatter 2-3 tablespoons flour over dough. Replace cover, turn processor on and a ball should form.) Process for 1 minute more to knead dough (stop the food processor immediately if dough catches and/or blade labors or stops).

Carefully remove dough from food processor. Place on a floured surface. Remove blade from processor and place processor bowl over dough, or cover with another bowl. Let dough rest for 10 minutes. Shape into a tapered loaf that will fit diagonally on a greased baking sheet. Cover with oiled wax paper and let rise in a warm place (80-85°F) until doubled in size. Brush loaf with water. Make diagonal slashes across the top of the loaf with a knife.

Preheat oven to 400°F. Bake for 30-35 minutes, until crust is golden brown and loaf has a hollow sound when tapped on the bottom. Remove bread from pan and cool on a wire rack. For a softer crust, brush crust lightly with melted butter or oil when the bread comes out of the oven.

BREAD MACHINE SOURDOUGH RECIPES

The following recipes are designed for 1½ pound loaves made using the "sweet bread" cycle. Adjustments may be needed for 1 pound loaf bread machines. At high altitudes, bread machine recipes may need to be adjusted to avoid over-rising of the dough. Using less yeast, adding a bit more salt, adding gluten and using a longer kneading cycle may help. For further help with bread machine adjustments for high altitude, see *Tips for Successful Bread Machine Baking* (page 119), or contact your local County Cooperative Extension Office (the number can be found in the phone book under "County Government").

BREAD MACHINE SOURDOUGH BREAD
Makes 1 Loaf

2	teaspoons active dry yeast (above 6,500 feet, decrease to 1½ teaspoons)
1½	teaspoons salt
1½	teaspoons gluten
¼	cup non-fat dry milk
1	tablespoon sugar
3	cups bread or all-purpose flour
1	tablespoon olive oil
1½	cups Basic Batter
½	cup + 1 tablespoon hot water (125°F)

Put yeast, salt, gluten, dry milk, sugar, flour and olive oil in bread machine. In a medium bowl, combine basic batter and water; add to bread machine. Follow bread machine instructions for baking bread.

BREAD MACHINE SOURDOUGH
OATMEAL BREAD
Makes 1 Loaf

2	teaspoons active dry yeast (above 6,500 feet, decrease to 1½ teaspoons)
1½	teaspoons salt
1½	teaspoons gluten
¼	cup non-fat dry milk
¼	cup potato buds or flakes
½	cup quick-cooking oats
1	tablespoon sugar
3	cups bread or all-purpose flour
2	tablespoons olive oil
1½	cups Basic Batter
¾	cup + 2 tablespoons hot water (125°F)

Put yeast, salt, gluten, dry milk, potato buds, oats, sugar, flour and olive oil in bread machine. In a medium bowl, combine basic batter and water; add to bread machine. Follow bread machine instructions for baking bread.

VARIATION: Substitute 2 cups whole-wheat flour for 2 cups of the bread or all-purpose flour. Increase gluten to 1½ tablespoons.

SOURDOUGH PANCAKES OR CRÊPES

Makes 10 to 12 Pancakes or 12 Crêpes

1	large egg
1	tablespoon milk
1	tablespoon butter, melted or vegetable oil
1	cup Basic Batter
¼	cup whole-wheat or all-purpose flour
1	tablespoon sugar
½	teaspoon salt
¼ ½	teaspoons baking soda (use ½ teaspoon for fluffier pancakes)

Preheat a griddle to 375°F or a skillet over medium-high heat. In a medium bowl, beat egg, milk and butter or oil. Stir in basic batter. In a separate bowl, sift or stir flour, sugar, salt and baking soda together; stir into the egg mixture. Ladle batter onto lightly greased griddle or a skillet. Cook pancakes until golden brown on both sides.

Crêpes: Omit flour and baking soda. Increase milk to 2 tablespoons. Heat a non-stick or a lightly greased skillet over medium-high heat until added drops of water "dance" and sizzle. Pour 2 tablespoons of batter onto the center of a 6-inch pan or 3 tablespoons of batter onto an 8-inch pan; quickly rotate the pan to spread the batter evenly over the bottom of the pan. Cook on one side only, until bottom is lightly browned with a lacy look. Loosen edges and carefully lift crêpe from pan to a plate.

SOURDOUGH BISCUITS

Makes 10 to 12 Biscuits

1½	cups Basic Batter
½	stick (¼ cup) + 2 tablespoons butter or margarine, melted
1¼	cups flour
1	tablespoon sugar
½	teaspoon salt
1	teaspoon baking powder
¼	teaspoon baking soda

Preheat oven to 375°F. Grease a 9x9-inch or 7x11-inch baking pan. Put basic batter in warm bowl; stir in ½ stick of melted butter. Combine flour, sugar, salt, baking powder and baking soda in a separate bowl; add to basic batter mixture and stir with fork until a soft dough is formed. Form dough into a ball and place on a lightly floured pastry cloth or board. Roll dough over and knead lightly 10-15 times. Roll or pat out dough to ½-inch thick. Cut with a biscuit cutter. Brush both sides of biscuits with the remaining 2 tablespoons of melted butter. Arrange biscuits close together in the pan. Bake for 15-20 minutes, or until golden brown.

SOURDOUGH APPLESAUCE OR CARROT CAKE

Makes One 9x13-inch Cake

1½	cups Basic Batter
¼	cup non-fat dry milk
1	cup applesauce or grated peeled carrot
¼	cup white sugar
½	cup packed brown sugar
2	large eggs, beaten
1	stick (½ cup) butter or margarine, softened
1	cup all-purpose flour
½	teaspoon salt
2	teaspoons baking soda
1	teaspoon cinnamon
½	teaspoon nutmeg
½	teaspoon allspice
¼	teaspoon ground cloves
½	cup chopped walnuts
1	cup raisins

Preheat oven to 350°F. Grease and flour a 9x13-inch baking pan. In a large bowl, combine basic batter, dry milk and applesauce or grated carrot. In a medium bowl, cream together white sugar, brown sugar, eggs and butter. In a third bowl, combine flour, salt, baking soda, cinnamon, allspice, cloves, nuts and raisins. Add the sugar mixture and the flour mixture to the basic batter mixture; beat well. Pour batter into pan. Bake for 30-35 minutes, or until a toothpick inserted in the center comes out clean.

SOURDOUGH BAGELS

Makes 8 Bagels

These bagels freeze well.

> 2½ cups all-purpose flour (up to 3 cups, if needed)
> 1 tablespoon active dry yeast
> 2 tablespoons + 1 tablespoon sugar
> ½ teaspoon salt
> 1 large egg, slightly beaten
> 1½ cups Basic Batter
> ½ stick (¼ cup) butter or margarine, melted or ¼ cup vegetable oil
> 4 cups + 1 tablespoon water
> 1 large egg white
> Sesame or poppy seeds (optional)

In a large bowl, combine ¾ cup flour and yeast. Stir in 2 tablespoons sugar, salt, egg and basic batter. Stir in melted butter. Beat for 2 minutes at high speed of a mixer (watch that the dough does not climb the beaters and get into the motor). Stir in enough of the remaining flour to make a stiff dough. Knead on a well-floured surface until smooth and elastic (dough can also be made in a stand mixer with a dough hook). Put dough in a lightly greased bowl, cover and let rise until doubled in size. Punch down. Divide dough into 8 pieces. Shape into balls and place on a greased baking sheet. Cover with wax paper and let rest for 15 minutes.

In a large pot, bring 4 cups water and the remaining 1 tablespoon of sugar to a boil. Poke a hole through each ball of dough with index finger, then twirl around finger to enlarge hole (it should look like donut). Set aside on a baking sheet; cover with wax paper. Preheat oven to 400°F. Slide bagels into boiling water, 3 or 4 at a time (don't crowd them). Simmer for 2 minutes per side, or until firm to the touch. Use the handle of a wooden spoon to prevent holes in bagels from closing. Drain bagels on paper towels (handle as little as possible – pressure can cause hard spots where partially cooked dough compresses).

Combine egg white and the remaining 1 tablespoon of water; brush over bagels. Sprinkle with sesame seeds or poppy seeds, if desired. Put bagels on a greased baking sheet. Bake for 15-20 minutes, or until deep golden brown.

SOURDOUGH PIZZA CRUST

Makes 1 Crust

1	cup Basic Batter
1	teaspoon salt
1	tablespoon vegetable oil or margarine, melted
1	cup all-purpose flour (about)

Preheat oven to 475°F. Mix together all ingredients, working in enough flour to form a dough that can be rolled out flat into a thin layer. Roll out dough to desired thickness. Put dough on an oiled baking sheet or a pizza stone. Bake for 5 minutes. Top crust with favorite toppings, then bake for 15-20 minutes, or until crust is golden brown and the cheese is melted.

SOURDOUGH PIE CRUST

Makes 2 Crusts

1½	cups sifted all-purpose flour
¾	teaspoon salt
¼	teaspoon baking soda
½	cup shortening
½	cup Basic Batter

Sift or whisk flour, salt and baking soda into a bowl. Cut in shortening. Stir in basic batter with a fork until dough clings together. Divide dough in half and form into 2 balls. Chill in refrigerator or freezer for 10 minutes. Roll each ball out to use in your favorite recipes.

COOKIES
FROM
A QUICK MIX

COOKIES MADE FROM THE BASIC COOKIE MIX ARE

- A short cut for busy cooks.
- Easy to prepare.
- Simple to store.
- A quick way to prepare sweets.
- A simple means to vary menus.
- A treat for family and friends.

COOKIES WILL BE A SUCCESS IF YOU

- Stir cookie mix with a fork and then measure it; spoon mix lightly into measuring cup – do not pack it.
- Blend ingredients with an electric mixer, wooden spoon or pastry blender.

STORING COOKIES

- Cool cookies before storing.
- Store crisp and soft cookies separately.
- Keep crisp cookies in a container with a loose cover.
- Keep soft cookies in a tightly covered container.
- If cookies tend to dry out, add a piece of orange or apple, changing it often.

STORING COOKIES IN THE FREEZER

- Cool cookies completely before freezing.
- Place cookies gently in a freezer bag or an airtight container; if fragile, arrange cookies in a container cushioned with waxed paper.
- Store cookies in freezer for as long as several months.
- Thaw cookies completely before removing from container.

Combine flour, dry milk, baking powder and salt. Sift together 2 times. In a large bowl (6 quart capacity or greater), soften shortening with a mixer at medium speed or a large wooden spoon. Gradually add sugar and continue mixing until light and fluffy. Gradually add flour mixture. Blend thoroughly at low speed or cut in with a pastry blender until mixture is the consistency of coarse cornmeal. Store mix airtight in a large container. The mix will keep for 3-4 weeks in a cool, dry place, or for a year in the refrigerator.

*For richer-flavored cookies, substitute butter for the shortening, however, the mix must then be kept refrigerated!

COOKIE MIX

For 20 cups mix	3,500-6,500 feet	6,500-8,500 feet	8,500+ feet
Sifted all-purpose flour	9 cups	9 cups	9 cups
Non-fat dry milk	3 cups	3 cups	3 cups
Baking powder	3 tablespoons	2 tablespoons + ¾ teaspoon	1 tablespoon + 1½ teaspoons
Salt	1 tablespoon	1 tablespoon	1 tablespoon
Shortening or margarine*	4 cups	4 cups	4 cups
sugar	4 cups	4 cups	4 cups

CHERRY DROPS *Makes 3½ to 4 Dozen (2-inch) Cookies*

3	cups Cookie Mix
2	large eggs
½	cup chopped pecans
½	cup coarsely chopped drained maraschino cherries

Preheat oven to 375°F. Thoroughly mix cookie mix and eggs. Stir in cherries and nuts. Drop by teaspoonsful onto an ungreased baking sheet. Bake for 10-12 minutes. Remove to a wire rack to cool.

LEMON DROPS *Makes 2½ Dozen (1½inch) Cookies*

2	cups Cookie Mix
1	large egg
1	tablespoon lemon juice
1½	teaspoons grated lemon zest

Preheat oven to 375°F. Thoroughly mix all ingredients. Drop by teaspoonsful onto an ungreased baking sheet. Bake for 10-12 minutes. Remove to a wire rack to cool.

SUGAR COOKIES *Makes 3 Dozen (1½inch) Cookies*

3	cups Cookie Mix
1	large egg
½	teaspoon almond extract

Preheat oven to 375°F. Thoroughly mix all ingredients. Roll out dough ⅛- to ¼-inch thick and cut with a cookie cutter. Put cookies on an ungreased baking sheet. Bake for 8-10 minutes. Remove to a wire rack to cool. Sprinkle with sugar or decorate as desired.

THUMBPRINT COOKIES _Makes 2½ to 3 Dozen (1½ inch) Cookies_

½	(8-ounce) package cream cheese, softened
2	cups Cookie Mix
¾	teaspoon vanilla extract
1	large egg white, slightly beaten
¾	cup finely chopped nuts
9	maraschino cherries, cut into quarters

Preheat oven to 350°F. Thoroughly blend cream cheese, cookie mix and vanilla. Roll into small balls, about 1 inch in diameter. Dip into slightly beaten egg white, then roll in nuts. Put dough balls on a greased baking sheet. Press top of each ball with your thumb to make an indentation. Bake for 10-12 minutes. Remove to a wire rack to cool. Place ¼ maraschino cherry in the center of each cookie.

PEANUT BUTTER COOKIES _Makes 7 Dozen (1½ inch) Cookies_

4	cups Cookie Mix
½	cup packed brown sugar
1	cup creamy or crunchy peanut butter
1	large egg
1½	teaspoons vanilla extract
2	tablespoons water

Preheat oven to 375°F. Thoroughly mix all ingredients. Roll dough into small balls, about 1 inch in diameter. Put dough balls on an ungreased baking sheet. Flatten balls with a fork. Bake for 10-12 minutes. Remove to a wire rack to cool.

CHOCOLATE CHIP COOKIES *Makes 5 Dozen (2-inch) Cookies*

4	cups Cookie Mix
1	large egg
¼	cup water
1½	teaspoons vanilla extract
¼	cup packed brown sugar
1	cup (6-ounce package) semisweet chocolate chips
1	cup chopped walnuts

Preheat oven to 375°F. Thoroughly mix cookie mix, egg, water, vanilla and brown sugar. Stir in chocolate chips and nuts. Drop by teaspoonsful onto an ungreased baking sheet. Bake for 10-13 minutes. Remove to a wire rack to cool.

OATMEAL COOKIES *Makes 3½ to 4 Dozen (2-inch) Cookies*

1	cup raisins
½	cup reserved raisin cooking water
2	cups Cookie Mix
1	cup quick-cooking oats
2	tablespoons packed brown sugar
½	teaspoon cinnamon
½	teaspoon allspice
1	large egg
1½	teaspoons vanilla extract
½	cup chopped walnuts

Preheat oven to 375°F. Cover raisins with water; bring to a boil, lower heat and simmer for 5 minutes. Drain raisins, reserving ½ cup of raisin cooking water. Thoroughly mix raisins, reserved raisin cooking water, cookie mix, oats, brown sugar, allspice, egg and vanilla. Stir in walnuts. Drop dough by teaspoonsful onto an ungreased baking sheet. Bake for 13-15 minutes. Remove to a wire rack to cool.

COCONUT SUPREME COOKIES

Makes 3 Dozen (1½ to 2-inch) Cookies

2	cups Cookie Mix
1	large egg
2	tablespoons water
1	teaspoon vanilla extract
1	cup shredded coconut
1	cup chopped walnuts

Preheat oven to 375°F. Thoroughly mix cookie mix, egg, water and vanilla. Stir in coconuts and walnuts. Drop by teaspoonsful onto a lightly greased baking sheet. Bake for 12-15 minutes. Remove to a wire rack to cool.

CRISP CHOCOLATE DROPS

Makes 3 to 3½ Dozen (1½inch) Cookies

4	ounces (4 squares) semisweet chocolate, melted
2	tablespoons water
2	cups Cookie Mix
1	teaspoon vanilla extract
½	cup chopped nuts

Preheat oven to 375°F. Thoroughly mix melted chocolate, water, cookie mix and vanilla. Stir in nuts. Drop by teaspoonsful onto an ungreased baking sheet. Bake for 10-12 minutes. Remove to a wire rack to cool.

VARIATIONS: Roll the dough into balls and roll in powdered sugar before baking – this gives the cookies a sweet, crinkled coating. Or, drizzle baked, cooled cookies with melted milk or white chocolate.

CINNAMON COOKIES *Makes 3½ Dozen (2-inch) Cookies*

2½ cups Cookie Mix
½ cup sugar
1 large egg
1 teaspoon vanilla extract
1½ teaspoons cinnamon
¼ cup finely chopped nuts

Preheat oven to 375°F. Thoroughly mix cookie mix, sugar, egg and vanilla. Form into balls, about 1½ inches in diameter. Combine cinnamon and nuts; roll balls in this mixture. Place balls 2 inches apart on an ungreased baking sheet. Bake for 12-15 minutes. Remove to a wire rack to cool.

MOLASSES COOKIES *Makes 5 to 6 Dozen (2-inch) Cookies*

4 cups Cookie Mix
¼ teaspoon ground cloves
½ teaspoon cinnamon
½ teaspoon ground ginger
1 large egg
¼ cup molasses

Preheat oven to 375°F. Blend all ingredients thoroughly. Refrigerate dough for 60 minutes. Roll chilled dough into balls, about 1½ inches in diameter. Place on a lightly greased baking sheet. Flatten dough balls with the bottom of a glass covered with a damp cloth. Bake for 8-10 minutes. Remove to a wire rack to cool.

PECAN BARS *Makes 4 Dozen (1x2-inch) Bars*

2	cups Cookie Mix
2	tablespoons water
1	large egg
	Topping (recipe follows)

Preheat oven to 375°F. Grease a 13x9-inch baking pan. Thoroughly mix cookie mix, water and egg. Spread into pan. Bake for 8-10 minutes. Lower oven temperature to 350°F. Spread topping on baked layer. Bake for 20-25 minutes more. Cool and cut into bars.

TOPPING	
2	large eggs
1	cup packed brown sugar
¼	cup Cookie Mix
½	teaspoon vanilla extract
1	cup chopped, halved or whole pecans, or more to your taste

Beat eggs until foamy. Add brown sugar, cookie mix and vanilla; mix thoroughly. Stir in the nuts.

CHEWY DATE NUT BARS *Makes 4 Dozen (1x2-inch) Bars*

2	large eggs
3	cups Cookie Mix
2	tablespoons water
¼	cup packed brown sugar
1	teaspoon vanilla extract
1	cup chopped pitted dates
1	cup coarsely chopped walnuts

Preheat oven to 350°F. Grease a 13x9-inch baking pan. Thoroughly mix eggs, cookie mix, water, brown sugar and vanilla. Stir in dates and walnuts. Spread into pan. Bake for 35-40 minutes. Cool and cut into bars.

DATE LAYER BARS *Makes 4 Dozen (1x2-inch) Bars*

3	cups Cookie Mix
1¾	cups quick-cooking oats
1	pound chopped pitted dates
1	tablespoon lemon juice
1½	cups + 2 tablespoons water
¼	cup packed brown sugar

Preheat oven to 350°F. Grease a 13x9-inch baking pan. Combine cookie mix and oats; press 2½ cups of this mixture into pan. Combine dates, lemon juice and water in a saucepan. Cook over low heat until the mixture is the consistency of thin jam; spread over mixture in pan. Mix brown sugar and the remaining 2 tablespoons of water into the remaining cookie mix mixture. Sprinkle over top of date layer; press down lightly. Bake for 30-35 minutes. Cool and cut into bars.

CRISPY BARS *Makes 20 to 30 (1¼x2-inch) Bars*

2	cups Cookie Mix
¼	cup + ¾ cup packed brown sugar
2	large eggs
¼	teaspoon salt
1	teaspoon vanilla extract
1	cup shredded coconut
1	cup crisp rice cereal
1	cup chopped walnuts or pecans

Preheat oven to 325°F. Grease a 9x9-inch baking pan. Combine cookie mix and ¼ cup brown sugar. Press into pan. Beat eggs until frothy. Stir in salt. Gradually add the remaining ¾ cup of brown sugar; beat until thick. Add vanilla, coconut, rice cereal and nuts; mix thoroughly. Spread over the mixture in the pan. Bake for 25-30 minutes. Cool and cut into bars.

BROWNIES *Makes 20 to 30 (1½x2-inch) Brownies*

6   squares (6 ounces) semisweet chocolate, melted
2   cups Cookie Mix
2   large eggs
¼   cup water
2   teaspoons vanilla extract
½   cup chopped walnuts

Preheat oven to 350°F. Grease and flour a 9x9-inch baking pan. Thoroughly mix melted chocolate, cookie mix, eggs, water and vanilla. Stir in walnuts. Spread into pan. Bake for 25-30 minutes. When slightly cool, cut into bars or squares.

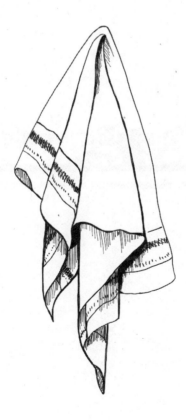

QUICK MIXES FOR CAKES, QUICK BREADS & MORE

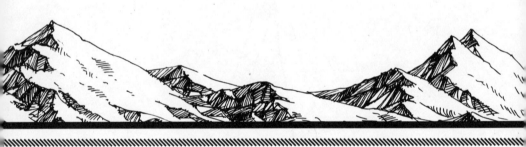

INTRODUCTION

The following all-purpose and cake mixes provide a shortcut for preparing a wide variety of baked goods, including biscuits, muffins, pancakes, waffles, breads, pastries, cakes and cookies. Generally, mixes prepared at home cost less than commercial mixes because you supply the labor! Shortening is used so that the mixes can be stored for convenient use. The all-purpose mix offers a range of salt and shortening amounts. The recipes were tested using the higher end of the range. However, good baked products that are lower in fat and sodium can be made using the lower end of the range. Substituting whole-wheat flour for part or all of the all-purpose flour in the all-purpose mix will increase the fiber content of baked goods. You can also substitute butter for shortening in the mixes, which will yield more flavorful baked goods, but the mixes must then be stored in the refrigerator!

The following tips will help ensure high quality products:
1. Spoon ingredients lightly into the cup and level with a spatula or the back of a knife. Be careful not to hit the side of the measuring cup, causing the dry ingredients to settle and measurements to be inaccurate.
2. Pack solid ingredients, such as vegetable shortening, firmly into a flushrim measuring cup so that no air pockets remain. A rubber spatula is useful to get all of the shortening out of the cup.
3. Always stir the mixes before measuring. Spoon lightly into a cup and level with a spatula or knife. Do not sift the mixes before using.
4. Store the mixes airtight in a glass jar, plastic container or freezer bag. If stored in an airtight container, the mixes will last for up to 6 months in a cool, dry location or up to 1 year in the refrigerator.
5. Storing mixes made with whole-wheat flour in the refrigerator or freezer helps prevent flavor changes due to the slightly higher fat content of whole-wheat flour.
6. Before storing the mix, label the container with the name of the mix, date prepared, use-by date and other information (such as your favorite recipe using the mix).
7. Recipes for all-purpose and cake mixes at three ranges of altitude are given. The names of the mixes reflect the type of flour used in preparing the mix. Each recipe specifies which mix to use.

Directions for preparing mixes: Combine flour, baking powder, salt and sugar; sift together 3 times into a large bowl. Cut in shortening with a pastry blender or two knives until mixture is the consistency of cornmeal. Store in an airtight container in a cool, dry place or in the refrigerator (the mix will last longer in the refrigerator, especially if using part or all whole-wheat flour in the All-Purpose Mix). These mixes will last for up to 6 months in a cool, dry location or up to 1 year in the refrigerator.

*Use all-purpose flour, whole-wheat flour or a mixture.
**For richer-flavored baked goods, substitute butter for shortening, except the mix must then be stored in the refrigerator!

ALL-PURPOSE MIX

For 11 cups mix	All-Purpose Mix 1 (3,500-6,500 feet)	All-Purpose Mix 2 (6,500-8,500 feet)	All-Purpose Mix 3 (8,500+ feet)
Flour (sift before measuring)*	9 cups	9 cups	9 cups
Baking powder	3 tablespoons	2 tablespoons + ¾ teaspoon	1 tablespoon + 1½ teaspoons
Salt	1-3 teaspoons	1-3 teaspoons	1-3 teaspoons
Sugar	¼ cup	¼ cup	¼ cup
Shortening**	1-2 cups	1-2 cups	1-2 cups

CAKE MIX

For 11 cups mix	Cake Mix A (3,500-6,500 feet)	Cake Mix B (6,500-8,500 feet)	Cake Mix C (8,500+ feet)
Cake flour (sift before measuring)	10 cups	10 cups	10 cups
Baking powder	2 tablespoons + 1½ teaspoons	1 tablespoon + 2 teaspoons	2½ teaspoons
Salt	1 tablespoon	1 tablespoon	1 tablespoon
Sugar	¼ cup	¼ cup	¼ cup
Shortening**	2 cups	2 cups	2 cups

BISCUITS *Makes 18 (2-inch) Biscuits*

3,500-6,500 feet: 3 cups All-Purpose Mix 1 or Cake Mix A
6,500-8,500 feet: 3 cups All-Purpose Mix 2 or Cake Mix A
8,500+ feet: 3 cups All-Purpose Mix 3 or Cake Mix B

OTHER INGREDIENTS
⅔   cup milk

Preheat oven to 450°F. Combine all-purpose or cake mix and milk; stir 25 strokes. Turn dough out onto a lightly floured surface; knead 15 times. Roll dough out ½-inch thick. Cut with a biscuit cutter. Transfer biscuits with a spatula to a greased baking sheet. Bake for 12-15 minutes.

VARIATIONS:
- CHEESE SWIRLS: Preheat oven to 425°F. Roll dough out into a ¼-inch thick, 18x11-inch rectangle. Sprinkle with 1 cup grated cheddar cheese. Roll dough up jelly-roll style and cut into ½-inch slices. Put slices, cut-side-up, on an ungreased baking sheet. Bake for 10-15 minutes.
- JELLY TRIANGLES: Preheat oven to 450°F. Roll dough out ¼ inch thick. Cut dough into 3-inch squares. On each square, place 1 teaspoon of tart jelly, such as raspberry. Fold squares diagonally and press edges together. Bake on an ungreased baking sheet for 12-15 minutes.
- FOR VARIETY IN SHAPES: Preheat oven to 450°F. Roll dough out ½-inch thick; cut into squares, triangles or other shapes. Combine 1 tablespoon cinnamon and ⅓ cup sugar; sprinkle on top of biscuits. Bake on a greased baking sheet for 12-15 minutes.

CINNAMON ROLLS *Makes 18 (2-inch) Biscuits*

3,500-6,500 feet: 3 cups All-Purpose Mix 1 or Cake Mix A
6,500-8,500 feet: 3 cups All-Purpose Mix 2 or Cake Mix A
8,500+ feet: 3 cups All-Purpose Mix 3 or Cake Mix B

OTHER INGREDIENTS
⅔	cup milk
¼	cup heavy cream
4	tablespoons butter, melted
1	tablespoon cinnamon
⅓	cup sugar
⅔	cup powdered sugar

Preheat oven to 450°F. Combine all-purpose or cake mix and milk; stir 25 strokes. Turn dough out onto a lightly floured surface; knead 15 times. Roll dough out ¼-inch thick. Combine cream and melted butter. Spread ½ of the cream mixture over the dough. Combine cinnamon and sugar; sprinkle over dough. Roll dough up jelly-roll style and cut into ½-inch slices. Bake on a greased baking sheet for 12-15 minutes. Mix powdered sugar into the remaining cream mixture. Spread over hot rolls after baking.

VARIATIONS: Substitute buttermilk for the milk. Also, sprinkle 1 cup of raisins or Craisins, more or less to taste, over the rolled out dough.

PEACH CAKE *Makes One 8x8-inch Cake*

3,500-6,500 fee: 1½ cups Cake Mix A
6,500-8,500 fee: 1½ cups Cake Mix B
8,500+ fee: 1½ cups Cake Mix C

OTHER INGREDIENTS
½   cup + 3 tablespoons sugar
½   cup milk
1   large egg
½   teaspoon vanilla extract
2   cups sliced peeled fresh peaches or well-drained,
    unsweetened sliced canned peaches
    Topping (recipe follows)
    Heavy cream (optional)

Preheat oven to 350°F. Grease an 8x8-inch baking pan. In a bowl, combine cake mix and sugar. In a separate bowl, combine milk, egg and vanilla. Pour ½ of milk mixture into cake mix mixture. Beat for 2 minutes with a mixer at low speed or 300 strokes by hand. Add remaining milk mixture. Beat for 2 minutes more at low speed or another 300 strokes. Spread ½ of batter into pan. Arrange peach slices on top of batter. Carefully spread remaining batter over peaches. Sprinkle topping over the batter. Bake for about 50 minutes, or until a toothpick inserted in the center comes out clean. Serve warm, with cream, if desired.

TOPPING
1   teaspoon grated lemon zest
⅓   cup sugar
½   teaspoon cinnamon
¼   cup chopped walnuts

Combine all ingredients.

BISCUIT APPLE CAKE *Makes One 8x8-inch Cake*

3,500-6,500 fee: 3 cups All-Purpose Mix 1
6,500-8,500 fee: 3 cups All-Purpose Mix 2
8,500+ fee: 3 cups All Purpose Mix 3

OTHER INGREDIENTS
¼ cup sugar
2 cups grated peeled apple*
2 teaspoons grated lemon zest
½ cup milk
1 cup raisins, Craisins or currants

Preheat oven to 350°F. Grease an 8x8-inch baking pan. Combine all-purpose mix and sugar. Add apple, lemon zest and milk; mix lightly. Stir in raisins, Craisins or currants. Spread batter into pan. Bake for about 45 minutes, or until a toothpick inserted in the center comes out clean. Serve warm with cream or ice cream.

*Use any apple that is crisp, sweet and juicy, such as Rome, golden delicious, Pink Lady or Fuji. For variety, substitute grated ripe pear for the apple and substitute 2 tablespoons of finely chopped candied ginger and 2 tablespoons of currants for ¼ cup of the raisins.

SHORTCAKE *Makes 1 Large Shortcake or 5 to 6 Individual Shortcakes*

3,500-6,500 feet: 3 cups All-Purpose Mix 1 or Cake Mix A
6,500-8,500 feet: 3 cups All-Purpose Mix 2 or Cake Mix A
8,500+ feet: 3 cups All-Purpose Mix 3 or Cake Mix B

OTHER INGREDIENTS
3   tablespoons sugar
½   cup milk
1   large egg
1-2   tablespoons butter or margarine, melted

Preheat oven to 425°F. Combine all-purpose or cake mix and sugar. In a separate
bowl, beat milk and egg with a whisk; add to all-purpose or cake mix mixture.
Stir with a fork until dry ingredients are just moistened, about 25 strokes. Knead
about 6 times on a lightly floured surface. Roll out dough about ½-inch thick.
Brush top of dough with melted butter or margarine. Cut dough in half. Place
one piece of dough, butter-side-up, on a baking sheet. Top with second piece,
butter-side-up. Bake for about 20 minutes, or until golden brown. Keep warm
until serving.

INDIVIDUAL SHORTCAKES: Cut rolled out dough into 10-12 rounds with a
3-inch biscuit or cookie cutter (use plain and/or decorative cutters of different
shapes). Brush top of each dough round with melted butter or margarine. Place
half of dough rounds, butter-side-up, on a baking sheet. Top with the remaining
rounds, butter-side-up. Bake for about 20 minutes, or until golden brown. Keep
warm until serving.

PEACH SHORTCAKE *Serves 5 to 6*

> 5-6   peaches, peeled and sliced (1 medium peach per serving)
> ⅓   cup sugar
> 1   recipe Shortcake (see page 160)
>   Butter, melted
>   Whipped cream (optional)

Gently toss peaches with sugar. Just before serving, separate layers of warm short-cake and spread with butter. Cover bottom layer with some of the peaches. Set top layer of shortcake in place. Top with remaining peaches (reserve some for garnish). Top with whipped cream, if desired. Garnish with reserved peaches.

STRAWBERRY OR RASPBERRY SHORTCAKE
Serves 5 to 6

> 3   pints strawberries or raspberries, hulled and washed
> ½   cup sugar, plus extra for garnish
> 1   recipe Shortcake (see page 160)
>   Butter, meted
>   Whipped cream (optional)

Reserve 6 of the largest strawberries or about 18 raspberries for garnish. Slice or crush remaining berries. Stir ½ cup sugar into berries. Let berries stand for 5 minutes. Sprinkle reserved berries with a little sugar.

Just before serving, separate layers of warm shortcake. Spread with butter. Cover bottom layer with some of the sugared berries. Set top layer of shortcake in place. Top with remaining berries. Top with whipped cream, if desired. Garnish with reserved berries.

MUFFINS WITH FOUR VARIATIONS *Makes 12 Muffins*

3,500-6,500 feet: 3 cups All-Purpose Mix 1 or Cake Mix A
6,500-8,500 feet: 3 cups All-Purpose Mix 2 or Cake Mix A
8,500+ feet: 3 cups All-Purpose Mix 3 or Cake Mix C

OTHER INGREDIENTS
2   tablespoons sugar
1   cup milk
1   large egg

Preheat oven to 425°F. Grease muffin cups. Combine all-purpose or cake mix and sugar. In a separate bowl, beat milk and egg together; add to all-purpose or cake mix mixture. Stir until dry ingredients are just moistened (the batter will be lumpy). Fill muffin cups ⅔-full. Bake for 20-25 minutes, until golden brown and firm to the touch.

VARIATIONS:
- SPICE CRUST MUFFINS: Mix 2 tablespoons sugar and ½ teaspoon cinnamon; sprinkle over muffin batter in muffin cups before baking.
- NUT, DATE OR PRUNE MUFFINS: Add ⅔ cup finely chopped nuts, dates or prunes to egg mixture before combining with all-purpose or cake mix.
- BLUEBERRY MUFFINS: Fold 1½ cups blueberries into batter before baking.
- JELLY MUFFINS: Pour muffin batter into muffin cups, filling cups ⅓-full. Put 1-2 teaspoons jelly, jam or preserves, such as raspberry or apricot, in the center of the batter in each muffin cup. Top with remaining batter, filling the cups ⅔-full.

PANCAKES OR WAFFLES *Makes 18 Pancakes or 6 Waffles*

3,500-6,500 fee: 3 cups All-Purpose Mix 1 or Cake Mix A
6,500-8,500 fee: 3 cups All-Purpose Mix 2 or Cake Mix A
8,500+ fee: 3 cups All-Purpose Mix 3 or Cake Mix C

OTHER INGREDIENTS
1½ cups milk
2   large eggs

Preheat griddle to 375°F or a skillet over medium-high heat. Put all-purpose or cake mix in a bowl. In a separate bowl, beat eggs and milk; add to all-purpose or cake mix and stir until blended. Pour or spoon batter onto lightly greased griddle or skillet. Cook pancakes until golden brown on both sides.

VARIATIONS:
- SOUR MILK PANCAKES OR WAFFLES: Mix 1 teaspoon baking soda into all-purpose or cake mix. Substitute 2 cups sour milk for the 1½ cups milk. (To make sour milk: mix 2 cups milk with 2 tablespoons lemon juice or distilled white vinegar; let stand for 5 minutes.)

DATE NUT COFFEE CAKE *Makes One 8x8-inch Coffee Cake*

3,500-6,500 fee: 2½ cups All-Purpose Mix 1 or Cake Mix A
6,500-8,500 fee: 2½ cups All-Purpose Mix 2 or Cake Mix A
8,500+ feet: 2½ cups All-Purpose Mix 3 or Cake Mix C

OTHER INGREDIENTS
½   cup sugar
1   large egg
½   cup milk
1   teaspoon vanilla extract
    Filling (recipe follows)

Preheat oven to 350°F. Grease an 8x8-inch baking pan. Stir all-purpose or cake mix and sugar together. In a separate bowl, beat milk, egg and vanilla; stir into dry ingredients until blended. Pour ½ of batter into pan. Spread filling over batter. Spread remaining batter over the filling. Bake for 40-45 minutes, or until a toothpick inserted in the center comes out clean.

FILLING
½   cup packed brown sugar
1   tablespoon flour
1   tablespoon cinnamon
½   stick (¼ cup) butter, melted
1   cup chopped pitted dates
½   cup chopped nuts

Mix all of the filling ingredients in a bowl. Or, for a smooth-textured filling, blend all of the filling ingredients in a blender or food processor.

CRUMBLE COFFEE CAKE *Makes One 8x8-inch Coffee Cake*

3,500-6,500 feet: 1¾ cups + 2 tablespoons All-Purpose Mix 1 or Cake Mix A
6,500-8,500 feet: 1¾ cups + 2 tablespoons All-Purpose Mix 2 or Cake Mix A
8,500+ feet: 1¾ cups + 2 tablespoons All-Purpose Mix 3 or Cake Mix C

OTHER INGREDIENTS
2   tablespoons lukewarm water (80-85°F)
1¼   teaspoons active dry yeast
½   cup + 3 tablespoons milk
2½   tablespoons sugar
1   large egg
¼   teaspoon vanilla extract
     Crumble topping (recipe follows)

Grease an 8x8-inch baking pans. Soften yeast in the lukewarm water. Heat ½ cup of milk just to the boiling point; remove from heat. Stir sugar into hot milk until dissolved; let cool to lukewarm. Add ½ cup all-purpose or cake mix to milk mixture; beat well. Add yeast, egg and vanilla; beat well. Add remaining mix; beat well until smooth. Cover and let rise in a warm place (80-85°F) until doubled in size.* Stir down. Spread batter into pan. Brush batter with remaining 3 tablespoons of milk. Sprinkle with crumble topping. Let rise until doubled in size.* Preheat oven to 375°F. Bake for about 30 minutes, or until a toothpick inserted in the center comes out clean.

*Approximate rising times at altitudes of:

	3,500-6,500 feet	6,500-8,500 feet	8,500+ feet
1st rising	50 minutes	25 minutes	10 minutes
2nd rising	25 minutes	17 minutes	12 minutes

CRUMBLE TOPPING
½   cup all-purpose flour
¼   cup dry bread crumbs
2   tablespoons sugar
½   teaspoon cinnamon
2   tablespoons butter or margarine, chilled

Combine flour, bread crumbs, sugar and cinnamon. Cut in butter or margarine until mixture is crumbly.

APPLE COFFEE CAKE

Makes One 9-inch Round or 8x8-inch Coffee Cake

3,500-6,500 feet: 1¾ cups + 2 tablespoons All-Purpose Mix 1 or Cake Mix A
6,500-8,500 feet: 1¾ cups + 2 tablespoons All-Purpose Mix 2 or Cake Mix A
8,500+ feet: 1¾ cups + 2 tablespoons All-Purpose Mix 3 or Cake Mix C

OTHER INGREDIENTS
2   tablespoons lukewarm water (80-85°F)
1¼   teaspoons active dry yeast
½   cup milk
2½   tablespoons + ¼ cup sugar
1   large egg
¼   teaspoon vanilla extract
3-4   medium apples, peeled and sliced
2   tablespoons butter or margarine, melted
1   teaspoon cinnamon

Grease a 9-inch round cake pan or 8x8-inch baking pan. Soften yeast in the lukewarm water. Heat milk just to the boiling point; remove from heat. Stir 2½ tablespoons sugar into milk until dissolved; let cool to lukewarm. Add ½ cup of all-purpose or cake mix to milk mixture; beat well. Add softened yeast, egg and vanilla; beat well. Add remaining mix; beat well until smooth. Cover and let rise in a warm place (80-85°F) until doubled in size.* Stir down. Spread batter into pan. Arrange apple slices on top of batter with slices overlapping. Brush with melted butter. Combine the remaining ¼ cup of sugar and cinnamon; sprinkle over apples. Let rise until doubled in size.* Preheat oven to 375°F. Bake for about 30 minutes, or until a toothpick inserted in the center comes out clean.

*Approximate rising times at altitudes of:

	3,500-6,500 feet	6,500-8,500 feet	8,500+ feet
1st rising	50 minutes	25 minutes	10 minutes
2nd rising	25 minutes	17 minutes	12 minutes

CRANBERRY SWIRL COFFEE CAKE

Makes One 9-inch Round Coffee Cake

3,500-6,500 feet: 1¾ cups + 2 tablespoons All-Purpose Mix 1 or Cake Mix A
6,500-8,500 feet: 1¾ cups + 2 tablespoons All-Purpose Mix 2 or Cake Mix A
8,500+ feet: 1¾ cups + 2 tablespoons All-Purpose Mix 3 or Cake Mix C

OTHER INGREDIENTS

2	tablespoons lukewarm water (80-85°F)
1¼	teaspoons active dry yeast
½	cup milk
2½	tablespoons + ¼ cup sugar
1	large egg
¼	teaspoon vanilla extract
½	cup whole berry cranberry sauce, preserves or marmalade
1	teaspoon cinnamon

Grease a 9-inch round cake pan. Soften yeast in the lukewarm water. Heat milk just to the boiling point; remove from heat. Stir 2½ tablespoons sugar into milk until dissolved; let cool to lukewarm. Add ½ cup of all-purpose or cake mix to the milk mixture; beat well. Add softened yeast, egg and vanilla to batter; beat well. Add remaining mix; beat well until smooth. Cover and let rise in a warm place (80-85°F) until doubled in size.* Stir down. Spread batter into pan. With a floured spoon, make grooves in a swirl design on top of batter. Fill grooves with cranberry sauce. Combine the remaining ¼ cup of sugar and cinnamon; sprinkle over batter. Let rise until doubled in size.* Preheat oven to 375°F. Bake for about 30 minutes, or until a toothpick inserted in the center comes out clean.

*Approximate rising times at altitudes of:

	3,500-6,500 feet	6,500-8,500 feet	8,500+ feet
1st rising	50 minutes	25 minutes	10 minutes
2nd rising	25 minutes	17 minutes	12 minutes

DATE NUT BREAD *Makes 1 Loaf*

3,500-6,500 feet: 2 cups All-Purpose Mix 1 or Cake Mix A
6,500-8,500 feet: 2 cups All-Purpose Mix 2 or Cake Mix B
8,500+ feet: 2 cups All-Purpose Mix 3 or Cake Mix C

OTHER INGREDIENTS

8	ounces whole dates, pitted and chopped (or about 12 large Medjool dates, pitted and chopped)
1	cup shredded coconut (optional)
½	cup sugar
⅔	cup boiling water
1	large egg, beaten
½	teaspoon vanilla extract
½	teaspoon baking soda (above 10,000+ feet, decrease to ¼ teaspoon)
½	teaspoon cinnamon
½	cup chopped nuts

Grease and flour a 9x5-inch loaf pan. Toss chopped dates and coconut with sugar. Pour boiling water over date mixture; stir and let cool. When cool, stir in beaten egg and vanilla. Preheat oven to 350°F. Combine all-purpose or cake mix, baking soda, cinnamon and nuts. Add date mixture to dry ingredients; mix until well blended. Pour batter into pan. Bake for about 60 minutes, or until a toothpick inserted in the center comes out clean.

BANANA BREAD *Makes One Loaf*

3,500-6,500 feet: 2 cups All-Purpose Mix 1 or Cake Mix A
6,500-8,500 feet: 2 cups All-Purpose Mix 2 or Cake Mix B
8,500+ feet: 2 cups All-Purpose Mix 3 or Cake Mix C

OTHER INGREDIENTS

¼	teaspoon baking soda
½	cup sugar
2	large eggs, beaten
1	cup mashed banana
2	tablespoons brandy or Grand Marnier (optional)
½	cup chopped walnuts or pecans (optional)

Preheat oven to 350°F. Grease and flour a 9x5-inch loaf pan. In a bowl, combine all-purpose or cake mix, baking soda and sugar. In a separate bowl, combine egg and banana; stir into dry ingredients until well blended. Stir in brandy and pecans, if desired. Pour batter into pan. Bake for about 60 minutes, or until a toothpick inserted in the center comes out clean.

VARIATION: Add 1 cup shredded coconut or 1 cup chocolate chips after adding the dry ingredients.

ORANGE RAISIN BREAD *Makes One Loaf*

3,500-6,500 feet: 2 cups All-Purpose Mix 1 or Cake Mix A
6,500-8,500 feet: 2 cups All-Purpose Mix 2 or Cake Mix B
8,500+ feet: 2 cups All-Purpose Mix 3 or Cake Mix C

OTHER INGREDIENTS	
	Peel and juice of 1 medium orange
½	cup boiling water (about)
1	cup raisins
1	large egg, beaten
1	teaspoon vanilla extract
1	teaspoon orange extract (optional)
¼	teaspoon baking soda
½	cup sugar

Preheat oven to 350°F. Grease and flour a 9x5-inch loaf pan, or line with parchment paper. Pour juice from orange into a measuring cup. Add enough boiling water to make ⅔ cup of liquid. Remove most of the white membrane from the orange peel. In a food processor fitted with the metal blade, grind orange peel and raisins. In a bowl, combine orange juice mixture and orange peel mixture. Add egg, vanilla and orange extract; mix well. In a separate bowl, combine all-purpose or cake mix, sugar and baking soda. Add orange juice mixture to dry ingredients; mix well. Pour batter into pan. Bake for about 60 minutes, or until a toothpick inserted in the center comes out clean.

APPLE PIE *Makes One 8-inch Pie*

```
1     recipe Pie Pastry (see page 171)
5-7   tart apples, peeled and thinly sliced*
¾-1   cup sugar (depending on desired sweetness)
2     tablespoons flour
1     teaspoon cinnamon
¼     teaspoon nutmeg
⅛     teaspoon salt
2     tablespoons butter
```

Preheat oven to 450°F. Put pie pastry into an 8-inch pie pan. Put apples in a bowl. Combine sugar, flour, cinnamon, nutmeg and salt. Add to sliced apples; toss to combine. Put apples in pie pan. Dot with butter. Top with top crust. Cut several vents into the crust. Bake for 10 minutes. Lower oven temperature to 350°F and bake for about 40 minutes more.

*NOTE: Gala, Fuji, Jonathan and Golden Delicious are all good choices for the apples. If the apples are not tart, toss sliced apples with 1 tablespoon lemon juice.

CHERRY PIE *Makes One 8-inch Pie*

```
1     recipe Pie Pastry (see page 171)
2     cups pitted cherries or canned pie cherries
⅓     cup cherry juice, or juice from canned pie cherries
⅛     teaspoon almond extract
⅔     cup sugar
3     tablespoon quick-cooking tapioca
1     tablespoon butter
```

Put pie pastry into an 8-inch pie pan. Combine cherries, cherry juice, almond extract, sugar and tapioca; let stand for 15 minutes. Pour into pie pan. Dot with butter. Make a lattice or twisted lattice top crust. Flute the crust edges. Preheat oven to 450°F. Bake for 10 minutes. Lower oven temperature to 350°F and bake for about 30 minutes more.

PIE CRUST *Makes Two 8-inch Crusts*

3,500-6,500 feet: 2 cups All-Purpose Mix 1
6,500-8,500 feet: 2 cups All-Purpose Mix 2
8,500+ feet: 2 cups All-Purpose Mix 3

OTHER INGREDIENTS
¼   cup butter, margarine, lard or shortening
¼   cup boiling water

Preheat oven to 450°F. Melt butter in the boiling water. Sprinkle over the all-purpose mix, blending with a fork. Turn dough out onto wax paper. Shape into a ball and wrap in the wax paper. Chill for at least 30 minutes. Roll out to use. For single crust pies, prebake for about 15 minutes (crusts for double crust pies (pies with a top crust) do not need to be prebaked).

FUDGE PUDDING *Makes One 8x8-inch Pudding*

3,500-6,500 fee: 1½ cups All-Purpose Mix 1 or Cake Mix A
6,500-8,500 fee: 1½ cups All-Purpose Mix 2 or Cake Mix A
8,500+ fee: 1½ cups All-Purpose Mix 3 or Cake Mix B

OTHER INGREDIENTS
½   cup sugar
¾   cup chopped nuts
2   tablespoons + ¼ cup unsweetened cocoa powder
½   cup milk
1   teaspoon vanilla extract
¾   cup packed brown sugar
1¾ cups boiling water

Preheat oven to 350°F. Combine all-purpose or cake mix, sugar, nuts and 2 tablespoons cocoa. Stir in milk and vanilla; beat well. Spread batter into an 8x8-inch baking pan. Combine brown sugar and the remaining ¼ cup of cocoa; sprinkle over batter. Pour boiling water over all – *do not stir!* Bake for 45-50 minutes, or until a toothpick inserted in the center comes out clean.

OATMEAL COOKIES *Makes 4 Dozen Cookies*

3,500-6,500 fee: 3 cups All-Purpose Mix 1 or Cake Mix A
6,500-8,500 fee: 3 cups All-Purpose Mix 2 or Cake Mix A
8,500+ fee: 3 cups All-Purpose Mix 3 or Cake Mix C

OTHER INGREDIENTS

1	cup firmly packed brown sugar
1	teaspoon cinnamon
¾	cup milk
1	large egg, beaten
1	cup old-fashioned rolled oats
1	cup chopped nuts
1	cup raisins, Craisins or chocolate chips, or a mixture

Preheat oven to 375°F. In a bowl, combine all-purpose or cake mix, sugar and cinnamon. In a separate bowl, combine milk and egg; stir into dry ingredients until well blended. Stir in oats, nuts and raisins, Craisins and/or chocolate chips. Drop by teaspoonsful onto a greased baking sheet. Bake for 12-15 minutes.

SUGAR COOKIES *Makes 4 Dozen (2½inch) Cookies*

3,500-6,500 fee: 3 cups All-Purpose Mix 1 or Cake Mix A
6,500-8,500 fee: 3 cups All-Purpose Mix 2 or Cake Mix A
8,500+ fee: 3 cups All-Purpose Mix 3 or Cake Mix C

OTHER INGREDIENTS

1	cup sugar
1	large egg, beaten
3-4	tablespoons milk
1	teaspoon vanilla extract

In a bowl, combine all-purpose or cake mix and sugar. In a separate bowl, combine egg, milk and vanilla; stir into dry ingredients until well blended. Chill dough thoroughly (2-3 hours or overnight).

Preheat oven to 375°F. On a lightly floured surface, roll dough out ⅛-inch thick. Cut into desired shapes. Sprinkle with white sugar, colored sugar, chopped nuts or other decoration. Bake on a greased baking sheet for 10-12 minutes, or until lightly browned.

GINGERSNAPS *Makes 5 Dozen Cookies*

3,500-6,500 feet: 4 cups All-Purpose Mix 1 or Cake Mix A
6,500-8,500 feet: 4 cups All-Purpose Mix 2 or Cake Mix A
8,500+ feet: 4 cups All-Purpose Mix 3 or Cake Mix C

OTHER INGREDIENTS
1   cup + ¼ cup sugar
1½   teaspoons ground ginger
½   teaspoon ground cloves
1   teaspoon cinnamon
1   teaspoon baking soda
2   large eggs, beaten
½   cup molasses, warmed slightly (aids mixing)

In a bowl, combine all-purpose or cake mix, 1 cup of sugar, ginger, cloves, cinnamon and baking soda. In a separate bowl, combine eggs and molasses; stir into dry ingredients until well blended. Chill dough thoroughly (2-3 hours or overnight).

Preheat oven to 375°F. Put the remaining ¼ cup of sugar on a plate. Shape dough into balls about 1 inch in diameter and roll in sugar. Put dough balls on a greased baking sheet and flatten with the bottom of a glass.

VARIATION: Instead of shaping dough into balls and rolling in sugar, roll out dough on a lightly floured surface to ¼-inch thick and cut with a cookie cutter. Sprinkle tops of cookies with the ¼ cup of sugar. Bake for 10-12 minutes.

CHOCOLATE CAKE *Makes Two 8-inch Layer Cakes*

3,500-6,500 feet: 3 cups Cake Mix A
6,500-8,500 feet: 3 cups Cake Mix A
8,500+ feet: 3 cups Cake Mix B

> OTHER INGREDIENTS
> 3   ounces (3 squares) unsweetened chocolate
> 1½   cups sugar
> 1⅓   cups milk
> 2   large eggs
> 1   teaspoon vanilla extract

Preheat oven to 375°F. Line the bottoms of two 8-inch round cake pans with wax paper, or grease and flour lightly. Melt chocolate; cool. In a large bowl, combine cake mix and sugar. In a separate bowl, combine milk, eggs and vanilla. Pour ¾ cup of the milk mixture into the cake mix mixture. Add the melted, cooled chocolate. Beat for 2 minutes with a mixer at low speed or 300 strokes by hand. Add the remaining milk mixture. Beat for 2 minutes more at low speed or another 300 strokes. Divide batter between the pans. Bake for about 30 minutes, or until a toothpick inserted in the center comes out clean.

YELLOW CAKE *Makes Two 8-inch Layer Cakes*

3,500-6,500 feet   3 cups Cake Mix A
6,500-8,500 feet   3 cups Cake Mix B
8,500+ feet   3 cups Cake Mix C

> OTHER INGREDIENTS
> 1⅓   cups sugar
> 1   cup milk
> 2   large eggs
> 1   teaspoon vanilla extract

Preheat oven to 375°F. Line the bottoms of two 8-inch round cake pans with wax paper, or grease and flour lightly. In a bowl, combine cake mix and sugar.

In a separate bowl, combine milk, eggs and vanilla. Pour ½ of the milk mixture into the cake mix mixture. Beat for 2 minutes with a mixer at low speed or 300 strokes by hand. Add the remaining milk mixture. Beat for 2 minutes more at low speed or another 300 strokes. Divide batter between the pans. Bake for about 30 minutes, or until a toothpick inserted in the center comes out clean.

WHITE CAKE *Makes Two 8-inch Layer Cakes*

3,500-6,500: feet 3 cups Cake Mix A
6,500-8,500: feet 3 cups Cake Mix B
8,500+ feet: 3 cups Cake Mix C

OTHER INGREDIENTS
1   cup + ¼ cup sugar
½   teaspoon almond extract
½   teaspoon vanilla extract
¾   cup milk
4   large eggs whites

Preheat oven to 375°F. Line the bottoms of two 8-inch round cake pans with wax paper, or grease and flour lightly. In a bowl, combine cake mix and 1 cup of sugar. In a separate bowl, combine almond extract, vanilla and milk. Beat egg whites until foamy. Gradually add the remaining ¼ cup sugar to the egg whites. Beat until egg whites are stiff and glossy (but not dry). Add ½ cup of the milk mixture to the cake mix mixture. Beat for 2 minutes with a mixer at low speed or 300 strokes by hand. Add the remaining milk mixture and the egg white mixture. Beat for 2 minutes more at low speed or another 300 strokes. Divide batter between the pans. Bake for about 30 minutes, or until a toothpick inserted in the center comes out clean.

ALTITUDE ADJUSTMENTS:
6,500-8,500 feet: Reduce the 1 cup of sugar to 1 cup less 1 tablespoon.
8,500+ feet: Reduce the 1 cup of sugar to 1 cup less 2 tablespoons.

BUTTERMILK CHOCOLATE CAKE

Makes Two 8-inch Layer Cakes

Using buttermilk produces a light cake with a fine, velvety texture.

3,500-6,500 feet: 3 cups Cake Mix A
6,500-8,500 feet: 3 cups Cake Mix A
8,500+ feet: 3 cups Cake Mix B

OTHER INGREDIENTS
3   squares unsweetened chocolate
1½   cups sugar
½   teaspoon baking soda
1⅓   cups buttermilk
2   large eggs
1   teaspoon vanilla extract

Preheat oven to 375°F. Line the bottoms of two 8-inch round cake pans with wax paper, or grease and flour lightly. Melt chocolate; cool. In a bowl, combine cake mix, sugar and baking soda. In a separate bowl, combine buttermilk, eggs and vanilla. Pour ¾ cup of the buttermilk mixture into the cake mix mixture. Add the melted, cooled chocolate. Beat for 2 minutes with a mixer at low speed or 300 strokes by hand. Add the remaining buttermilk mixture. Beat for 2 minutes more at low speed or another 300 strokes. Divide batter between the pans. Bake for about 30 minutes, or until a toothpick inserted in the center comes out clean.

CHERRY UPSIDE DOWN CAKE *Makes One 8x8-inch Cake*

3,500-6,500 fee: 1½ cups Cake Mix A
6,500-8,500 fee: 1½ cups Cake Mix B
8,500+ fee: 1½ cups Cake Mix C

OTHER INGREDIENTS
½   cup + 3 tablespoons sugar
½   cup milk
1   large egg
½   teaspoon vanilla extract
    Cherry filling (recipe follows)

Preheat oven to 350°F. Grease an 8x8-inch baking pan. In a bowl, combine cake mix and sugar. In a separate bowl, combine milk, egg and vanilla. Pour ½ of the milk mixture into the cake mix mixture. Beat for 2 minutes with a mixer at low speed or 300 strokes by hand. Add the remaining milk mixture. Beat for 2 minutes more at low speed or another 300 strokes. Pour cherry filling into pan. Pour cake batter over filling. Bake for 40-45 minutes, or until a toothpick inserted in the center comes out clean. Cool slightly and then invert onto a plate while still warm.

CHERRY FILLING
⅓   cup sugar
1½   tablespoons cornstarch
1¼   cups (½ of a 14-ounce can) sour red cherries, drained
     (syrup reserved)

Combine sugar and cornstarch in a saucepan. Add reserved syrup from cherries and cook until thick and clear. Stir in cherries.

PEACH UPSIDE DOWN CAKE *Makes One 8x8-inch Cake*

3,500-6,500 fee: 1½ cups Cake Mix A
6,500-8,500 fee: 1½ cups Cake Mix B
8,500+ fee: 1½ cups Cake Mix C

OTHER INGREDIENTS

½	cup + 3 tablespoons sugar
½	cup milk
1	large egg
½	teaspoon vanilla extract
2	cups canned peach slices or halves, drained (syrup reserved)
3	tablespoons butter or margarine
⅔	cup reserved syrup from canned peaches

Preheat oven to 375°F. Grease an 8x8-inch baking pan. In a bowl, combine cake mix and sugar. In a separate bowl, combine milk, egg and vanilla. Pour ½ of the milk mixture into the cake mix mixture. Beat for 2 minutes with a mixer at low speed or 300 strokes by hand. Add the remaining milk mixture. Beat for 2 minutes more at low speed or another 300 strokes. Arrange peach slices or halves close together in the pan.

Cook reserved peach syrup over medium heat until thick. Add butter and stir until melted and combined; pour over peaches. Pour cake batter over peaches. Bake for 40-45 minutes, or until a toothpick inserted in the center comes out clean. Cool slightly and then invert onto a plate while still warm.

PINEAPPLE UPSIDE DOWN CAKE *Makes One 8x8-inch Cake*

3,500-6,500 fee: 1½ cups Cake Mix A
6,500-8,500 fee: 1½ cups Cake Mix B
8,500+ fee: 1½ cups Cake Mix C

OTHER INGREDIENTS

½	cup + 3 tablespoons sugar
½	cup milk
1	large egg
½	teaspoon vanilla extract
½	stick (¼ cup) butter or margarine
⅔	cup packed brown sugar
9	slices canned, unsweetened pineapple
9	maraschino cherries

Preheat oven to 375°F. In a bowl, combine cake mix and sugar. In a separate bowl, combine milk, egg and vanilla. Pour ½ of the milk mixture into the cake mix mixture. Beat for 2 minutes with a mixer at low speed or 300 strokes by hand. Add the remaining milk mixture. Beat for 2 minutes more at low speed or another 300 strokes.

Melt the butter in an 8x8-inch baking pan in the oven. Remove the pan from oven. Add the brown sugar to the butter in the pan; stir to combine. (Be careful – the pan will be hot!) Arrange pineapple slices on top of the butter mixture. Put a maraschino cherry in the center of each pineapple slice. Pour cake batter over fruit. Bake for 40-45 minutes, or until a toothpick inserted in the center comes out clean. Cool slightly and then invert onto a plate while still warm.

Recipe	# of Servings	Cal.	Prot. (g)	Carb. (g)	Fbr.(g)	Fat (g)	Sat. Fat (g)	Chol. (mg)	Sod. (mg)
Mile High Cakes									
Buttermilk Chocolate Cake	1 slice; 1/20	266	3.2	33.4	1.4	14.1	4	28	195
Chocolate Raspberry Cake	1 slice; 1/12	461	6.1	69.7	1.8	18.6	11.4	87	132
Hot Fudge Kahlúa Cake	1 slice; 1/16	175	1.8	34.5	1.2	2.7	1.6	6	113
Chocolate Cake	1 slice; 1/16	199	2.9	24.9	0.4	10.2	1	35	55
Chocolate Sour Cream Cake	1 slice; 1/16	135	3.3	27	0.4	2.2	1.3	3	29
Cocoa Frosting	3½ tablespoons	122	0.5	22.4	0.2	4.2	0.9	0	47
Tropical Cake	1 slice; 1/18	311	4.2	43.6	1.1	13.7	6.8	35	256
Angel Food Cake	1 slice; 1/18	96	3	21.1	0.1	0	0	0	72
Chiffon Cake	1 slice; 1/18	164	2.8	22.9	0.3	6.8	0.5	30	42
White Cake	1 slice; 1/16	176	2.4	26.1	0.4	6.5	0.3	0	113
Yellow Cake	1 slice; 1/16	246	3.5	35.5	0.5	10.2	2.6	35	26
Banana Cake	1 slice; 1/12	329	4.3	47.4	0.7	14.4	1.9	41	104
Oatmeal Cake	1 slice; 1/16	182	3.4	32.8	1.3	4.4	0.9	52	159
Coconut Frosting	2 tablespoons	133	1.5	9.3	1.5	8.2	3.9	0	46
Burnt Sugar Cake	1 slice; 1/16	203	2.6	34.7	0.4	6.1	1.5	35	123
Burnt Sugar Frosting	4 tablespoons	153	0.4	25.9	0.0	5.8	1.1	0	107
Burnt Sugar Cake	1 slice; 1/16	203	2.6	34.7	0.4	6.1	1.5	35	123
Whole Wheat Carrot Cake	1 slice; 1/24	211	3.4	30.1	1.8	9.5	2.1	50	90
Dark Fruit Cake	1 slice; 1/75	99	1.5	18.9	1.2	2.6	0.5	0	25
Applesauce Cake	1 slice; 1/16	221	3.5	31	2.2	10.2	0.8	35	93
Warm Apple Torte	1 slice; 1/12	169	1.8	27	0.7	6.2	4.2	31	143
Raspberry Walnut Torte	1 slice; 1/15	244	2.8	35	1	10.6	4.8	41	144
Holiday Cranberry Cake	1 slice; 1/16	109	1.8	19.3	0.9	2.8	1.3	16	141
Chocolate Carrot Cake	1 slice; 1/18	402	3.7	52.1	1.5	21	8.1	57	345
Carrot Cake	1 slice; 1/16	271	4.2	37.8	1.5	11.9	0.9	70	102
Chocolate Zucchini Cake	1 slice; 1/18	356	4.8	42.6	2.1	20	7.1	34	284
Pineapple Cake	1 slice; 1/20	296	3.9	33.9	2.3	16.9	5.6	30	175

Recipe	# of Servings	Cal.	Prot. (g)	Carb. (g)	Fbr.(g)	Fat (g)	Sat. Fat (g)	Chol. (mg)	Sod. (mg)
Buttermilk Chocolate Cake	1 slice; 1/20	266	3.2	33.4	1.4	14.1	4	28	195
Cookies, Bar Cookies & Biscotti									
Conejos Cookies	1 cookie; 1/72	110	1	12	0.5	6.7	2.7	9	77
Mocha Chip Cookies	1 cookie; 1/96	78	0.9	11	0.4	3.7	2.4	9	48
Banana Choc. Chip Cookies	1 cookie; 1/24	235	4	35.3	2.3	10	6.2	28	166
Basic Drop Cookie	1 cookie; 1/66	46	0.6	6	0.1	2.2	0.6	8	43
Carrot Raisin Cookies	1 cookie; 1/48	51	1.2	7.9	0.6	1.8	0.4	6	34
Oatmeal Cookies	1 cookie; 1/66	56	1	6.7	0.5	2.9	0.6	4	24
Zucchini Cookies	1 cookie; 1/48	70	1	9.5	0.7	3.3	0.7	6	33
Decadent Choc. Shortbread Bars	1 bar; 1/32	163	1.7	20.7	0.3	8.2	5.8	20	68
Fruit Nut Energy Bars	1 bar; 1/36	109	2.6	15.8	1.2	4.5	0.6	15	71
Apple Raisin Bars	1 bar; 1/36	106	1.3	16.7	0.5	4	0.6	15	69
Applesauce Dream Bars	1 bar; 1/36	79	1.6	12.1	0.8	2.8	0.5	0	45
Honey Almond Biscotti	1 biscotti; 1/48	62	1.3	9.6	0.7	2	0.1	0	166
Chocolate Chip Biscotti	1 biscotti; 1/24	84	1.8	15.6	0.6	1.8	0.8	23	108
Quick Breads, Coffee Cakes & Muffins									
Megan Miller's Pumpkin Bread	1 slice; 1/15	236	3	33.3	1.5	11	1.3	25	209
Whole Wheat Quick Bread	1 slice; 1/15	188	4.5	27.7	2	7.1	1.4	19	120
Zucchini Carrot Bread	1 slice; 1/15	145	3	16.4	1.7	8.3	1.1	37	111
Basic Quick Bread – Cake	1 slice; 1/15	194	2.9	26.7	0.9	8.6	1.3	56	112
Banana Quick Bread – Muffin	1 slice; 1/15	155	2.9	23	1	5.9	0.9	38	120
Gingerbread	1 slice; 1/16	140	2.7	18.7	0.6	6.1	0.5	35	10
Raspberry Almond Coffee Cake	1 slice; 1/15	244	2.8	35	1	10.6	4.8	41	144
Pear Walnut Coffee Cake	1 slice; 1/8	601	7.8	82.5	3.7	28	13.4	70	520
Quick Coffee Cake	1 slice; 1/8	284	5.1	43.7	1	10	1.8	37	263
Applesauce Coffee Cake	1 slice; 1/16	175	2.6	29	2.1	6.4	1.1	17	150
Muffins	1 muffin; 1/12	149	3.4	21	0.7	5.6	1	25	163
Strawberry Choc. Chip Muffins	1 muffin; 1/18	188	3.2	27.1	1.1	7.8	5	45	152
Pumpkin Muffins	1 muffin; 1/24	244	3.9	29.4	1.3	12.9	3.8	29	199

Recipe	# of Servings	Cal.	Prot. (g)	Carb. (g)	Fbr.(g)	Fat (g)	Sat. Fat (g)	Chol. (mg)	Sod. (mg)
Morning Glory Muffins	1 muffin; 1/15	274	4.1	38.2	2.3	11.7	7.4	59	337
Blueberry Cream Muffins	1 muffin; 1/12	286	3.7	34.5	1	14.5	4.6	45	203
Scones, Cornbreads, Biscuits, Pancakes & More									
Apricot Streusel Scone	1 scone; 1/12	176	3.4	23.8	1.1	7.5	4.8	49	192
Raisin Streusel Scone	1 scone; 1/12	174	3.3	23.3	1.1	7.5	4.9	49	194
Cranapple Scone	1 scone; 1/8	331	5.4	38.3	1.6	17.4	10.5	69	486
Cornbread	1 slice; 1/9	181	5.2	27.4	1.9	5.4	1.2	65	375
Southwestern Jalapeño Cornbread	1 slice; 1/9	265	10.3	2.1	7.5	9.7	4.1	66	500
Southern Buttermilk Cornbread	1 slice 1/16	98	3	15.7	1.3	3	0.6	27	242
Biscuits	1 biscuit; 1/15	100	2.2	13.4	0.6	4.1	1.1	1	124
Pancakes	1 pancake; 1/8	115	3.2	14.7	0.5	4.8	0.9	37	203
Oatmeal Pancakes	1 pancake; 1/10	98	3.7	12.2	1.5	4.2	0.8	29	113
Toasted Apricot Almond Pancakes	1 pancake; 1/4	485	11.5	5	40.6	19.8	7.4	73	457
Cake Doughnuts	1 doughnut; 1/14	242	2.9	22.7	0.7	15.8	2.1	21	136
Crêpes	1 crêpe; 1/7	76	4.6	9	0.2	2.3	0.5	42	99
Cream Puffs	1 puff; 1/18	76	2.1	6.1	0.2	4.7	2.5	71	67
Flour Tortillas	1 tortilla; 1/11	128	2.4	17.3	0.7	5.3	1.3	0	232
Popovers	1 popover; 1/11	78	3.1	10.2	0.4	2.7	0.8	52	90
Making Yeast Breads at High Altitude									
White Bread	2 slices; 1/18	202	5.3	36.3	1.5	3.6	0.4	0.4	272
White Bread Enriched with Soy Flour & Wheat Germ	2 slices; 1/18	143	4.4	25	1.3	2.8	0.3	0.3	203
Whole Wheat Bread	2 slices; 1/18	212	7.4	37.4	4.7	4.9	0.5	0.5	274
Herb Bread	2 slices; 1/12	174	4.6	30.7	1.3	3.2	0.4	20.8	304
Rye Bread	2 slices; 1/9	240	5.1	44	1.8	5.2	0.6	0	388
French Bread	2 slices; 1/18	150	4.5	31.3	1.4	0.4	0	0	262
Onion Herb Braid	1 slice; 1/15	277	7.4	42.3	2.1	8.4	4.8	69	300
Honey Wheat Bread	1 roll; 1/24	191	7.1	37.1	3	2.2	1.3	5	269
Bavarian Snitzbrod	1 slice; 1/42	203	5.5	36	4.2	4.8	1.8	19	78

Recipe	# of Servings	Cal.	Prot. (g)	Carb. (g)	Fbr.(g)	Fat (g)	Sat. Fat (g)	Chol. (mg)	Sod. (mg)
Dilly Bread	1 slice; 1/30	106	4.5	18.1	0.9	1.7	0.8	16	238
Focaccia	1 piece; 1/15	154	2.7	18.7	0.9	7.6	1	0	311
Quick No-Knead Batter Bread	2 slices; 1/9	205	6.2	35.3	1.6	4.1	0.6	27.8	280
English Muffin Bread	2 slices; 1/18	160	5.3	32.9	1.4	0.4	0	0.5	273
Basic Yeast Roll	1 roll; 1/42	77	2.1	12.9	0.6	1.7	0.3	11.8	62
Basic Roll Dough Cinnamon Rolls	1 roll; 1/42	95	2.2	0.7		2.6	0.4	11.8	72
Whirligig Rolls	1 slice; 1/9	118	0.4	18.1	0	5.4	1.1	0	68
Sugar Crumb Coffee Cake	1 slice; 1/9	79	0.9	8.5	0.3	4.8	0.7	0	32
Cinnamon Blossom Coffee Cake	1 slice; 1/9	113	0.8	0.2		3.8	0.6	0.1	100
Coconut Pineapple Coffee Cake	1 slice; 1/9	75	0.2	6.2	1.1	5.8	2.3	0	49
Orange Coffee Cake	1 slice; 1/9	67	0.2	7.9	0.3	4.0	0.8	0	49
Crumble Squares	1square; 1/9	57	0.7	7.3	0.2	2.8	0.6	0.1	51
Honey Topping Coffee Cake	1 slice; 1/9	116	0.4	18.1	0	5.1	1	0	65
Refrigerator Yeast Rolls	1 roll; 1/42	108	2.7	18.8	0.7	2.4	0.6	14	62
Parmesan Cracked Wheat	2 slices; 1/9	187	7	34.4	3.6	3.1	0.7	1.8	157
Almond Breakfast Bread	1 slice; 15	218	6	39.7	1.2	3.2	1.3	4	298
Today's Sourdough at High Altitude									
White Bread	1 slice; 1/18	103	2.9	20.1	0.7	0.9	0.2	0	75
Sourdough Refrigerator Rolls	1 roll; 1/36	113	2.8	20.1	0.7	2.2	0.2	0	68
Sourdough Honey Wheat Bread	1 slice; 1/18	118	2.6	21.6	0.7	2.2	0.4	0	88
Sourdough Herb Bread	1 slice; 1/18	98	2.3	16.6	0.6	2.2	0.4	0	73
Bread Machine Sourdough Bread	1 slice; 1/18	121	3.6	0.8	2.2	1.1	0.1	0	199
Bread Machine Oatmeal Bread	1 slice; 1/18	138	3.9	25.6	1.2	2	0.2	0	200
Sourdough Pancakes or Crêpes	1 pancake; 1/12	59	1.8	8.8	0.3	1.8	0.3	17	138
Sourdough Biscuits	1 biscuit; 1/12	136	2.8	20.7	0.7	4.3	0.8	0	160
Applesauce or Carrot Cake	1 slice; 1/18	205	3.3	30.4	1.7	8	1.4	23	239
Bagels	1 bagel; 1/8	300	8.1	49.6	1.9	6.9	1.3	25	226
Sourdough Pizza Crust	1 slice; 1/8	118	3	21.5	0.8	1.9	0.6	1	291
Sourdough Piecrust	1 slice; 1/12	148	2.2	15.2	0.5	8.4	3	5	162

Recipe	# of Servings	Cal.	Prot. (g)	Carb. (g)	Fbr.(g)	Fat (g)	Sat. Fat (g)	Chol. (mg)	Sod. (mg)
Recipes from a Quick Mix									
Cherry Drops	1 cookie; 1/45	69	1.2	7.6	0.3	3.8	0.8	9	49
Lemon Drops	1 cookie; 1/30	54	1	6.3	0.1	2.8	0.7	6	46
Sugar Cookies	1 cookie; 1/36	67	1.2	7.8	0.1	3.4	0.9	5	57
Thumbprint Cookies	1 cookie; 1/33	80	1.5	6.9	0.3	5.4	1.5	4	52
Peanut Butter Cookies	1 cookie; 1/84	63	1.6	6.5	0.3	3.5	0.8	2	49
Chocolate Chip Cookies	1 cookie; 1/60	81	1	8.7	0.4	4.9	1.4	4	43
Oatmeal Cookies	1 cookie; 1/48	61	1	8.1	0.5	2.8	0.6	4	379
Coconut Supreme Cookies	1 cookie; 1/36	63	1.1	6	0.3	3.8	1.1	5	42
Crisp Chocolate Drops	1 cookie; 1/39	65	1.1	6.8	0.3	3.8	1.1	0	34
Cinnamon Cookies	1 cookie; 1/39	67	1.1	8.7	0.2	3.1	0.7	5	44
Molasses Cookies	1 cookie; 1/66	54	1	6.8	0.1	2.4	0.6	3	45
Pecan Bars	1 bar; 1/48	75	1.2	9.2	0.3	3.9	0.7	12	37
Chewy Date Nut Bars	1 bar; 1/48	82	1.5	10	0.5	4.3	0.8	8	45
Date Layer Bars	1 bar; 1/48	90	1.4	15.8	1.1	2.7	0.7	0	43
Crispy Bars	1 bar; 1/25	156	2.3	19.5	0.6	7.9	2.4	15	103
Quick Mixes for Cakes, Quick Breads & More									
Biscuits	1 biscuit; 1/18	119	2.1	13.4	0.5	6.2	1.5	0	148
Biscuits – Cheese Swirls	1 biscuit; 1/18	145	3.6	13.5	0.5	8.2	2.9	7	187
Cinnamon Rolls	1 roll; 1/18	186	2	21.3	0.7	10.4	4.4	12	156
Biscuit Apple Cake	1 biscuit; 1/8	212	2.9	34.8	1.3	7.1	1.7	0	170
Peach Shortcake	1 shortcake; 1/6	492	7.5	68.1	3.3	21.2	6	37	449
Raspberry Shortcake	1 shortcake; 1/6	532	8	77	9.7	21.8	6	37	449
Strawberry Shortcake	1 shortcake; 1/6	517	7.8	73.4	4.9	21.7	6	37	451
Shortcake	1 shortcake; 1/6	407	6.9	46.1	1.4	21.1	6	37	449
Muffins	1 muffin; 1/12	195	3.8	22.5	0.7	9.6	2.4	16	230
Muffins – Spice Crust	1 muffin; 1/12	203	3.8	24.7	0.7	9.6	2.4	16	230
Muffins – Blueberry	1 muffin; 1/12	202	3.9	24.3	1	9.7	2.4	16	230
Pancakes	1 pancake; 1/18	131	3.1	14	0.5	6.7	1.7	21	160

Recipe	# of Servings	Cal.	Prot. (g)	Carb. (g)	Fbr.(g)	Fat (g)	Sat. Fat (g)	Chol. (mg)	Sod. (mg)
Waffles	1 waffle; 1/6	392	9.3	42.1	1.4	20	5	64	480
Date Nut Coffee Cake	1 slice; 1/16	247	2.7	37.3	1.2	10.2	3.4	20	148
Crumble Coffee Cake	1 slice; 1/16	137	2.6	17.5	0.6	6.2	2.1	16	125
Apple Coffee Cake	1 slice; 1/16	135	1.9	18.4	0.9	6.1	2.1	16	108
Cranberry Swirl Coffee Cake	1 slice; 1/16	122	1.9	18.1	0.5	4.6	1.2	12	111
Date Nut Bread	1 slice; 1/16	179	2.5	26.9	1.7	7.4	1.5	12	151
Banana Bread	1 slice; 1/16	132	2.1	19.3	0.7	5.2	1.3	23	134
Orange Raisin Bread	1 slice; 1/16	145	2	23.7	0.7	5	1.2	12	132
Apple Pie	1 slice; 1/8	385	3	54.1	2.7	18.1	7.7	23	252
Cherry Pie	1 slice; 1/8	345	3.2	46.8	1.4	16.5	6.7	19	217
Pie Pastry	1/8	224	2.6	19.3	0.7	14.9	5.8	15	215
Fudge Pudding	1 serving; 1/16	173	2.5	25.8	1.3	7.4	1.4	0	90
Oatmeal Cookies	1 cookie; 1/48	74	1	8.9	0.5	4.1	0.8	4	72
Sugar Cookies	1 cookie; 1/48	40	0.2	4.6	0	2.4	0.6	4	55
Gingersnaps	1 cookie; 1/60	40	0.2	5.4	0.1	2	0.5	6	67
Chocolate Cake	1 slice; 1/8	446	6.3	67.2	2.1	18.5	6.7	48	351
Yellow Cake	1 slice; 1/8	371	4.9	59.4	0.5	12.6	3.2	47	344
White Cake	1 slice; 1/8	257	5	32	0.5	11.5	2.9	0	353
Buttermilk Chocolate Cake	1 slice; 1/8	448	6.2	67	2.1	18.8	6.9	48	451
Cherry Upside Down Cake	1 slice; 1/16	114	1.3	20.4	13.6	3.2	0.8	12	86
Peach Upside Down Cake	1 slice; 1/16	130	1.5	19.6	13.2	5.3	2.1	18	88
Pineapple Upside Down Cake	1 slice; 1/16	173	1.4	29.4	23.1	6.1	2.6	20	90
Peach Cake	1 slice; 1/16	130	1.7	21.7	14.9	4.4	0.9	12	86

INDEX

NOTES